'My encounters with Amelia Dalton have been mostly on the high seas near places like Madagascar, Borneo and Venezuela, where she has proven time and again her ingenuity, resilience and courage. Now I know how this mix of attributes came to reside in one extraordinary person. *Mistress and Commander* is exuberant, heart-warming and inspiring, a captivating read.'

Lee Durrell

'Imagine A Year in Provence with the cast of Para Handy; add a touch of James Herriot, and you'll get the drift of *Mistress and Commander*. Imagine Freya Stark, or some other dauntless female, taking on the alpha male communities of maritime Scotland and you'll have the measure of Amelia Dalton.'

Peter Hughes, travel writer

For ten years, **Amelia Dalton** owned a small ship running cruises to the remote island chains of Scotland's stunning West Coast. She worked closely with The National Trust for Scotland, and gained her commercial qualifications as a Captain. Amelia now advises individual clients on river and ocean cruises and runs her own travel company, Amelia Dalton Travel.

Mistress
and
Commander

Amelia Dalton

SANDSTONEPRESS
HIGHLAND | SCOTLAND

First published in Great Britain and the
United States of America

Sandstone Press Ltd
Dochcarty Road
Dingwall
Ross-shire
IV15 9UG
Scotland

www.sandstonepress.com

This book is based on actual events. Some names have been
changed to protect the privacy of the individuals involved.

The publisher acknowledges subsidy from Creative Scotland
towards publication of this volume.

ISBN: 978-1-910985-17-5
ISBNe: 978-1-910985-18-2

Cover design by David Wardle at Bold and Noble
Typeset by Iolaire Typography Ltd
Printed and bound by CPI Group (UK) Ltd, Croydon, CR0 4YY

To my wonderful, supportive son, Hugo and in memory of his little brother Digby.

Acknowledgements

I owe many, many thanks to the people who enabled these events to take place and this book to exist. My then-husband, John for his early enthusiasm and financial wizardry, the shareholders for their finance, Kate for her stalwart strength, Cubby who taught me of the sea and whose jokes I shall never forget, Peter Hughes for his unceasing encouragement and patience, and finally, Moira at Sandstone Press for her unwavering help and advice.

All of you changed my life.

One

It was January 1989, the day of my father-in-law's funeral and I was late. I hurried downstairs, past portraits of glaring ancestors and the armorial stained-glass window, resisting the urge to run. That would be considered unseemly. As I reached the bottom step, the ancient black Bakelite telephone, lurking on a linen chest, tinkled into life.

I knew I was already unpopular with my mother-in-law for not being ready and waiting in the drawing room and I really did *not* want to answer the insistent ringing. The grey, dead light of a winter afternoon in Yorkshire seeped through the chilly hunting lodge, packed with the great and good of the county come to pay their respects. If I answered the urgent ringing, as well as incurring my mother-in-law's ire, my fierce sisters-in-law would accuse me, the future mistress of the estate, of taking over. Yet I couldn't just ignore it; no doubt it would be someone wanting to offer condolences.

'Could I speak to John Dalton?' a woman's crisp voice asked.

'I'm afraid he's busy,' I said. 'This is Amelia, his wife. Can I give him a message?'

'I'm ringing about his boat,' the woman continued. 'Could you tell him there's a problem? I'm told it's sinking in the North Sea and an oil rig has had to be closed down.'

'I'm sorry, but you must have the wrong—' I stopped. What was she talking about? It dawned on me: we did have a boat, which we'd owned for all of two days. How could it be sinking already?

People were pouring past me, through the hall and on into the library, the drawing room, the study, filling up the house. My father-in-law had been much loved in the village and respected by all. He was a staunch churchman who had enjoyed a distinguished career as a major-general. Tall and handsome even in his eighties, he had been High Sheriff of Yorkshire, and possessed the quiet strength of those who have successfully negotiated war and command, dealt with family crises and village in-fighting, horses, shoots, hunts and dogs, as well as running London Zoo.

The high-ceilinged Victorian rooms were packed by now as I went looking for my husband, John. Eventually I found him. True to form, he wasted no time asking questions such as why was the boat sinking, but simply told me: 'Sort it out, Amelia, but do it quietly.'

I had only seen what was to become 'our' boat once, when we had gone to check it out in Denmark, and I knew it was a powerful machine. We'd bought an Arctic trawler, built for working in frozen seas, eighty-five feet of solid oak. How could it be sinking? There were people on board – what about them? Shutting down an oil rig sounded horribly expensive.

I had no idea what to do. I was a middle-class Yorkshire girl with a background in antiques and cooking, the daughter of a judge, happily married with two little boys and an unruly springer spaniel.

I needed advice from the man we had engaged as our future skipper, Cubby MacKinnon. He was whiling away the days, as he waited for his new command, by keeping a fancy yacht warm through the winter. He, his wife, Kate and the yacht were tucked away in a remote village on Scotland's west coast. I went back to the hall and rang his village pub fully expecting him to be there, propping up the bar. Surprisingly, he was not. The barman, in typically helpful west coast style, sent someone to find him. I waited, listening to faint sounds of laughter from the other end. Suddenly Cubby's soft Highland tones came down the line into the hall. He listened to the little I could tell him. 'Find a shipyard,' was his succinct response.

Find a shipyard during a funeral party from the middle of the Yorkshire Pennines! I started with the basics – Directory Enquiries. Surprisingly, they gave me a number. But suspicion met me as I tried to sound knowledgeable about getting a large boat out of the sea. One yard after another made it quite clear they weren't interested, each one fobbing me off with another shipyard's number, but I ploughed on. In a flash of inspiration, I offered to pay the next one up front, using John's gold Amex card. And so it was that a shipyard in a place curiously called 'Fraserburgh' became moderately willing to help.

3

'Yes,' I said gratefully, 'she'll be with you tomorrow. This is her call sign – Mike Hotel Alpha Zulu 8.' I hoped I sounded professional.

Twenty minutes later I had made my excuses and was in the car, heading away from the ancestral pile along the gravel drive, leaving behind the tea and scones of the wake. It was dark, the road was icy, and I knew I had to get over the Pennines to the north-east corner of Scotland where it seemed I would find Fraserburgh. It looked a good way north of Aberdeen, so I must have at least a six- or seven-hour drive, and I needed to go via Glasgow to reach the west coast to collect Cubby and Kate. I settled into my seat and focused on the road as it wound away up Wensleydale, empty in the winter Pennine dark. My little car had been christened the *Flying Tomato* by Hugo, our older boy. The two boys, Hugo and his younger brother, Digby, had clambered into the back seat, giggling with excitement at being able to sit in a car with no roof, and they loved the Ferrari red. 'Mummy, this is a flying tomato and we're the seeds!' Hugo had exclaimed and so the little Ford Escort XR3i had been the *Flying Tomato* ever since. Digby, enjoying the open roof, proudly called it our 'topless' car.

It was fun to drive, fast and responsive. I pressed the button for CD number three on the multi-disc player. Crystal Gayle crooned out from the dashboard, sweeping me on through the frosty night. I put my foot down; I needed to fly. I knew the boys would be happy and safe with Granny, and John was anxious for some good news.

The *Flying Tomato* slid on patches of ice on the

4

unfenced moorland road. Sheep, sleeping on the tarmac for warmth, loomed out of the dark like grey lumps snow. I swerved to avoid them; hitting one would definitely slow me down. Now, though, I had time to reflect, as I worked my way through a bar of chocolate, how a sunny summer cruise to the magnificent archipelago of St Kilda five years earlier had led to this slippery winter dash. Marine mortgages, business expansion schemes, development loans, shareholders and curious machinery: they all loomed much like the sheep and would have to be negotiated just as carefully, I would learn. But I felt excited.

Ticking off the miles, the motorway sliced through central Glasgow. I paid the toll for the Erskine Bridge crossing over the River Clyde, and began to wind my way along the cold black shores of Loch Lomond. Crystal Gale was getting repetitive but I was focusing on the twists and sharp bends of the road on this icy January night. On the straighter stretches I could push on and we swooped over the Rest and Be Thankful mountain pass, dropping down towards Inveraray. The sky was starry and frosty, but the road over the pass was well gritted and there were no cars to slow me down: the *Flying Tomato* sped along. Six hours after leaving Yorkshire, we slithered around the last tight bend into the tiny canal-side hamlet of Crinan. I parked close to the pub tucked under the hillside where I had called Cubby, and grabbing a torch from the glove pocket made my way across the glittering grass. No mobiles then, just a cold call box with a clammy black handset whiffing strongly of fish. I gave John a quick ring to report on progress.

5

After the snug warmth of the *Flying Tomato*, the chill of the phone box cut through my weariness and when John told me the news, I was sharply awake. His office had called again. It seemed our trawler, glamorously named *Monaco*, had been declared a full-scale emergency. However, John, typically resourceful, had found a tug and instructed the captain, whatever the swells and seas of January, to find her wherever she was in the North Sea, and to rescue her. But even this had not been enough: the *Monaco* was sinking too fast to get to Fraserburgh. The lifeboat had been called out too and now she was now being towed by the lifeboat into Peterhead. 'That's about thirty miles north of Aberdeen and so not as far as Fraserburgh. Get there,' John said, 'as quick as you can. I've spoken to Adrian and he's on his way too.' Relief flooded through me. I'd met Adrian, our marine surveyor, a couple of times. He'd done the final survey of the *Monaco* before we bought her. He knew about boats and the sea, and he would be there in Peterhead.

I ran across the slippery wooden lock gates, anxious not to waste time. There was the flimsy white yacht with Cubby and Kate, who were on their umpteenth coffee, killing time. But they were ready to go and I was thankful their funds hadn't run to a dram to ease the boredom of the wait.

Squeezing into the *Flying Tomato*, we headed off into the dark. I settled in for another five hours of twisty roads, but this time I had company. Cubby was ensconced in the front seat, quietly teasing tobacco out of a plastic pouch to roll a skimpy cigarette, and Kate – over six foot two of her – was curled up in the back, a large bottle of Irn-Bru wedged next to her proclaiming her Glaswegian origins. It was good to see them and hear their news. I knew none of the people they talked about, but the miles clocked up faster and the *craic* was entertaining.

'Do you think his survey was a load of rubbish?' I asked anxiously after a while, keen to have Cubby's view. 'Do you think she's just a tub full of holes?'

'No, I reckon she's OK. But there's a wee problem somewhere,' Cubby said.

Finally, after six hours of driving, I eased the trusty *Tomato* downhill into the granite port of Peterhead. The thin light of a bleak winter morning lit the blank, faceless walls of the top-security prison glowering over the town and the air was thick with a smell of treacle and fish. With its Branston pickle factory and tight-knit Baptist community of resilient, monosyllabic fishermen, Peterhead would become a vital part of my life. Over the years to come I learnt what made the town buzz, but right now I needed to negotiate the narrow streets leading down to the harbour and find our boat. Kate had never seen her, and Cubby and I only briefly three weeks earlier.

Exhaustion, momentarily gone in the excitement of arriving, now washed through me like an outgoing tide as I stopped the car. In the half-light of a dreich January morning, we peered through the windscreen towards a dense mass of trawlers tied up three or four deep along the quays. We searched for the *Monaco*. All I could see was a forest of steel struts and masts. In due course I learnt they were radar scanners, VHF aerials, whalebacks (deck shelters), rigging, trawl doors, A-frames and gallows. Cubby, totally at home in this apparently chaotic muddle, gently reminded me that she would have been pulled up out of the water to stop her sinking, so we needed to find the slipway. A working port landing hundreds of tons of fish every morning would not countenance a sinking boat in the harbour: the *Monaco* would be well out of the way, not hindering the urgent movements of the trawler fleet.

The harbour had five interconnecting basins, linked with narrow channels and swing bridges, and in the furthest corner from the sea was a large open area with sections where five ships could be pulled up out of the water. And there she was. There was the *Monaco*, looking totally unlike anything around her: like a fish out of water. She was not a trim, purposeful navy blue or black Scottish fishing machine, with tidy decks and neatly stowed fishing machinery. She was a bulky, tangled, smashed up mess. And her hull was painted the palest, daintiest, most delicate sky blue. She was, after all, Danish and the Danes painted all their fishing boats sky blue. You need a few tricks to ensure a big catch and a light blue hull merges into the dips and troughs of the swells, the spray and the mist, and you become invisible. A canny skipper can fish where he likes, secretly and unnoticed.

As well as looking completely out of place, *Monaco* seemed to writhe like an ant heap. People swarmed all over her. Men were underneath her, hammering at the hull, and there were more on deck, hacking at the twisted, broken fishing gear. Another bunch looked down from the wheelhouse windows forty feet above. I stood on the sloping concrete, staring up at the activity in a state of disbelief as again I wondered about the survey and whether this workforce was simply covering up inadequacies we should have known about.

Cubby leant against the harbour wall, again rolling a cigarette, eyeing up this mess that was supposed to be his future command. When he'd last seen her, she had at least been floating. Kate stood rigid beside him, staring, not moving a muscle, at the pale blue hull. A month ago she had signed on as cook and mate and this was her first introduction to her future life.

Monaco loomed over the wet, windswept slipway, high above us. She looked huge. But she was not threatening, already she almost seemed a bit of a friend, if a demanding one.

A lugubrious face peered out of a wheelhouse window: our surveyor, Adrian. He waved and made his way slowly down the ladder, joining us on the sloping concrete.

'Hello! When did you get here?' I could feel Cubby eying him up and knew he was wondering about the survey too. But when he and I had seen her we'd been sure she was not just a rotten hulk unable to keep out the sea. Cubby wandered off and slowly worked his way around underneath the hull, studying the planking.

'Adrian, please could you tell everyone to stop? We'd like to have a look round,' I said as firmly as I could manage.

'But every moment she's on the slip, up out of the water, is really costly. There's no point in wasting any time,' he protested.

I glanced across at Cubby, who by now been all

round under the hull and was resolutely studying his roll-up.

I persisted. 'Yes, of course you're right, thanks. But all the same, please can you tell everyone to stop working and take a break. I'd just like to take a moment to see what's what.'

Not waiting for an answer, I took a deep breath and put my foot on the first rung of the ladder stretching up the *Monaco*'s side. Thirty foot above, it was lashed to the gunwale and as I started to climb, it dipped and flexed each time I moved. Eyes watched from across the harbour, from under the hull and down from the deck. I climbed gingerly upwards. I was really tired and my legs were wobbly and stiff after the drive. I just kept going steadily, hand over hand. Up and up. The ladder bounced more and more as the others started up behind me. Eventually I reached the top and flung a leg over the gunwale, virtually falling on to the damaged deck. Carefully I worked my way around the torn, twisted metal and broken fishing gear which formed a steel cat's cradle over the deck, making my way over to the port side: I could just remember the layout.

I allowed myself a little grin. I'd made it — I was standing in the wheelhouse.

Two

It was all my father's fault.

In 1983, six years before my father-in-law's death, I had been sorting out the larder at our home in the tidy little garden suburb of Barnes when the phone interrupted me.

'Oh, Papa, it's you, how nice. How are you?'

'All well here.' He sounded as positive as ever. 'How are things with you? How is Digby?' He could always tell when I was a bit low, and Digby found even the early summer warmth difficult. 'Yes, it is extremely trying, I know. But it's time you and John had a break. Digby will be fine. You've not left him day or night for almost four years. It will be good for you. I've chartered a small boat for a week on the west coast of Scotland. The highlight will be visiting St Kilda.'

'Papa, I've never heard of St Kilda and I really don't want to leave Diggers.' I was not the slightest bit keen, but he was used to getting his own way.

Diggers, as he was always known, was our second son. Hugo, the eldest, had burst into the world, pink, happy and bouncing fit, like a miniature Buddha, but

11

Digby had been frail from the start and I had known something was not right. He was smiley, and usually happy, but at times was clearly in pain and I seemed unable to help. He was regularly drenched in sweat and often overheated. Feeding him was difficult too and he was horribly thin. Four years of ceaseless hospital investigations had come up with nothing. None of the experienced medics at Great Ormond Street Hospital had an answer. He'd fought pneumonia three times, his skin was thin and fragile and at the age of four he was still unable to walk. I spent every moment of every day, and most of every wakeful night, trying to figure it out. But he was also utterly endearing and rewarding. He was very bright, delightfully musical, had a glorious giggle and a disarming smile. 'You're not going anywhere! You're staying here with me!' he would say when I bent down to kiss him goodnight, locking a thin arm around my neck. I was lucky to have wonderful help in the pretty Sarah, whom the boys adored and who was as calm as I was frantic. She loved the boys but was rather less sure of our springer spaniel, Conker.

John, rather to my surprise, had agreed with my father. A break would do us both good and so, with much trepidation, we had left the boys in Yorkshire with John's efficient mother and major-general father in charge. But once we got to Scotland I knew I'd be out of communication, bobbing around in a boat way out in the Atlantic.

As we travelled north, my mother told me, 'As you know, Amelia, I've travelled all over the world with your father, and really, the west coast of Scotland still remains the most beautiful place I've ever been.'

The two of them had travelled widely, to New Zealand, Capri, Dubrovnik and Sicily. They had stayed at the Cipriani Hotel in Venice and in glorious private chateaux in the Medoc attending glamorous wine parties, so it seemed curious she regarded Scotland so highly. As my mother wittered on, I pretended to be dozing. I had a good excuse after hours in the rattling so-called 'sleeper' from London.

I gazed out at the hills as the train trundled towards Oban. They really were a soft heathery purple and the wild irises beside the track made spectacular splashes of gold. It was a perfect early summer's morning in June and my first visit to Scotland. We were an ill-assorted party of twelve. No one knew everyone. Glancing around the carriage, I surreptitiously tried to size them up. In Oban we were to join the boat chartered to take us to what had once been Britain's most remote island community – the jewel in the crown of the Scottish National Trust – the lonely archipelago of St Kilda. My father and his chum Viscount Livesey were involved in raising money to support the Trust's projects there and felt they should visit the island and learn first-hand why it mattered.

It was my thirty-first birthday but even the champagne at breakfast had made little difference to my mood. I felt utterly miserable at leaving the boys, wondering if Diggers would be OK and whether Sarah would remember to check on him every hour through the night as I did. My charismatic, charming gynae-cologist, Dickie, who had delivered Digby and now sat opposite me, nodding off, had insisted I should have bubbly for breakfast. Disapproval tinged with envy had oozed from every smoke-reeking pore of the elderly waiter in the station hotel at Glasgow Central, and in the Victorian gloom the early risers had been shocked at the sight of bubbly at seven a.m. I was still not sure what had made me suggest to Dickie and his wife, Sarah, that they might like to come with us. We had been practising a whip finish on a particularly pretty Green Highlander double-hooked salmon fly we were learning to tie at evening classes in Putney when the idea had come to me. And so here they were. They seemed happy enough, but who could tell?

A five-minute walk from the ornate station in Oban took us to the quay. Gulls strutted through fishy puddles, a big black-and-red car ferry loomed over the fishing boats tied up two or three deep alongside the pier. I followed along behind the viscount, wondering if we were in the right part of the harbour, then he stopped at the edge by a gaggle of trawlers and peered down. Twenty feet below, in deep shade, was a small black boat. I had been looking forward to a sleek white yacht, with smart teak deck furniture and cushions neatly piped and plumped, maybe a matching deck awning, and of course a sexy crew of bronzed hunks in white shorts and blue jerseys. Instead there was a scruffy old fishing boat, its deck awash with plastic carrier bags, and no one to be seen. No crew bustling about, no welcome party. We all peered over the edge, looking into the shadows below.

A tousled head with balding patch was suddenly stuck out of a window. 'You've arrived. Come on

14

down. Can you manage the ladder? Tide's awful low just now.' I stood back, waiting for one of the men to go first, to see how it was done. My turn. I plucked up courage and launched myself over the edge of the quay onto the top rung of the ladder, leaning out over the twenty-foot drop while I hung onto a bar set into the concrete and started down the vertical ladder. As I neared the boat the man grasped my arm to make sure I didn't slip as I stretched across the gap between the ladder and the side of the boat. Rather to everyone's surprise, we were soon all standing safely on the deck. The man flicked his cigarette into the water.

'Hullo, I'm Cubby. I'll not shake hands – they're a wee bit oily.' I wondered whether Veronica, the immaculate girl I had barely spoken to, had an oily handprint on the sleeve of her cashmere jersey. He turned towards a woman now standing on deck: she looked equally tousled.

'This is my wife, Kate. I'm glad you're not late. The forecast's good, a variable 3, so we'll be off in just a wee while.' He was quite short, with a neat little beard and a thin line of hair as a moustache along his upper lip. He looked bouncy and compact, light on his toes and completely in command. There was no air of deference to the viscount or to any of us, the charterers standing on his deck. Kate was a good six inches taller and looked a solid, no-nonsense type, with short spiky blonde hair. She smiled welcomingly and told us we'd find crisps and yoghurt in the saloon. Then she scampered up the ladder to deal with the cache of luggage waiting on the quay.

We stood about awkwardly, trying not to get in the

way, as between them Cubby and Kate roped down our bags; soon these nestled amongst the cardboard boxes and bulging carrier bags which littered the deck. Weetabix, UHT milk, digestive biscuits and a catering-sized pack of banana yoghurts snuggled up to tins of baked beans. None of it looked very encouraging.

'Katie! Are you there? Here's your fish,' a voice shouted from above. More boxes were roped down, this time with sandwiches labelled 'crab' and 'prawn' and finally two silvery salmon came swinging down on string looped through their mouths and gills. Papa squeezed about moving amongst the provisions, carefully studying the cardboard boxes. I knew he was searching to make sure the ones stamped *Wine Society* had arrived.

Seeing the others going inside the little boat, I followed, stepping up into a cramped passage. The others had all disappeared along the deck and, like everyone else, John and I needed to bag a cabin. We ended up with the smallest, immediately at the bottom of the vertiginous ladder-like stairs. It had two small bunk beds, three shelves fitted across a corner and a minute washbasin. I could just stand upright if I squeezed in alongside the bunks. All the cabins opened off the narrow barely lit passageway and people edged politely past each other, manoeuvring about to get their bags into their cabins. It all felt like boarding school at the start of a new term.

'Darling, whatever kind of boat is it? You never said it would be like *this*!' Veronica screeched. There was a mumbled reply from her companion Vernon, clearly well practised in absorbing her criticisms.

16

A steady rhythmic vibration began. Scrambling hand over hand up the ladder, I lurched over the high metal step and out onto the deck. In the midday sunshine with a cool breeze, the *Conochbar* had left the quay and was nosing out from between the fishing boats. Curious heaped-up chain-link contraptions stuck menacingly over their sides but she squeezed past without touching anything, turning away from the trawlers and the huge black and white ferries with *Caledonian MacBrayne* stamped along their sides. I stood in the bow and watched the hills above the town grow as we moved out into the harbour. The deck shook slightly under my feet and our boat turned to point towards open water.

Oban, compact with its prim little station and neat Victorian houses circling the bay, was to become the beginning and end of countless voyages. It was a view I would come to welcome. But for now I had not the slightest indication that from the first beat of the engine, my life had changed. My first experience of the west coast and my life at sea had begun.

John, calm as ever, stood chatting to Dickie. My mind drifted back to the boys, wondering again how they were. Glancing up at the windows of the wheel-house high above the deck I could see Cubby was at the wheel, Kate standing next to him. I waved cheerfully and then felt rather silly as neither waved back. I realised they were doing whatever you needed to do to get out of harbour on a busy sunny weekend at lunchtime in June. Ahead, there was an imposing fortress-like castle and a little lighthouse like a tiny white exclamation mark; both were dwarfed by the magnificent hills.

Scotland. It was just as I had imagined: it really did look like a picture on a biscuit tin.

Our party of twelve was made up of the viscount's six and my father's six. Viscount Livesey, a Yorkshire friend of Papa's, with his wife, Patsy, had brought their four friends: a journalist called Veronica with her absorbent boyfriend, Vernon, and an elegant couple who it seemed had their own yacht. Not, I suspected, like this workaday trawler, as they lived in the Canaries and owned a banana plantation. They had brought their house flag with them and now a bright yellow curved banana on a pale blue background fluttered incongruously beside the radar on the *Conochbar*'s stumpy mast.

We cruised up the Sound of Mull heading north-west. Little villages and white cottages dotted the shores, and it all looked idyllic in the warm sunshine as we ate our sandwiches on deck. After about three hours, the coast fell away behind and out in open waters the deck began to lift, much to my delight. It was like being at the fair.

'Hello! Can I come in, please?' I knocked on the wheelhouse door.

'Aye, in you come. There's not much of a seat, but you're very welcome.' I squeezed in and sat down quietly on the port side. 'That's Ardnamurchan light.' Cubby pointed to a big white lighthouse standing out on a rocky promontory. There were bumps of other islands, smoky blue and hazy in the distance. 'Those'll be the Small Isles, Canna, Rum, Eigg and Muck,' he went on, seeing where I was looking. 'And that's Skye away over there with the high hills. They're the Cullins;

18

they just rip the arse out of the clouds! That's why it rains so much.' I giggled at the graphic description. It all seemed pretty with the sea a soft blue. Maybe my mother had been right after all.

Fourteen hours after leaving Oban we arrived at the island of North Uist in the Outer Hebrides. We'd been rocked to sleep after a surprisingly delicious dinner of salmon and plum crumble, not a sign of the banana yoghurt, while our floating home had steamed steadily across the open waters of the Minch. Cubby had told us we'd be allowed ashore and, as the boat neared the quay in the little port of Lochmaddy, Dickie announced he'd been at medical school with the doctor who had kindly offered us the use of his car. The four of us jumped in; Dickie knew the island well from previous holidays spent fishing amongst the tiny lochs spattered amongst its flat, peat bog terrain. He headed the car across the island towards the beaches on the western side until we found ourselves looking again at the sea, at the open Atlantic with nothing between us and America, only our destination, St Kilda, way out there in the soft misty distance. The beach stretched away into the distance: right and left, pure and white, it stretched, unrolling like a ribbon, as far as I could see.

'Where's Dickie disappeared to?' I asked, turning to John who was sitting on a tuft of grass taking off his socks.

'Wha-hay!' A naked man hurtled past me down the beach and plunged into the waves. Dickie! Starkers! It was usually he who saw me with not much on, not the other way round. Sarah was snuggled down into her Barbour jacket with clearly no intention of joining him. Three of us, trousers hitched up, paddled rather primly along in the strand while Dickie swam way out into the silvery sea.

Cubby's strictures about boat behaviour and timing had been unequivocal: we knew not to be late and we also knew by now that Cubby was God. The skipper is always God, but Cubby had made his command quite clear from the moment we had stepped onto the deck of 'his' boat. We could join him in the wheelhouse and he had joined us for a dram after dinner, but whilst we might have chartered the boat, viscounts, surgeons, judges, journalists and financial wizards were all to dance to Cubby's tune.

'There's one of you not here!' he growled as we climbed down the ladder to get back on board. 'You were to be back for four and it's now fifteen past.' Above the sound of the engine, John shouted, 'Veronica's squatting in the pub!' As Dickie had parked the car, Veronica, swathed in a Hermes headscarf, had stalked past us, going in the opposite direction away from the quay.

'Just orff to the pub, darlings!' she shouted over her shoulder. 'I'm totally constipated at the sight of that loo! And how could anyone possibly call it a bathroom?' Now, she was just visible, as she sauntered slowly along.

'Buck up or the gap'll be too wide!' John called, standing on the gunwale with hand outstretched as the *Conochbar* steadily moved backwards. Cubby hung out of the wheelhouse window, watching, a roll-up firmly clamped between his lips as he judged the slowly widening gap. He winked and took the cigarette out of his mouth, pointed at me and then at the seat beside him. No one else had seen; all eyes had been on Veronica and the carefully judged widening gap.

John pulled her over the gunwale and inelegantly she fell onto the deck. Cubby knew exactly how to make it difficult but not impossible even in high heels.

The route out to St Kilda, between the islands of North Uist and Harris, was tricky to navigate and shallow so our boat could only make the passage at the right state of tide. Most boats, I later learned, avoided the route, deeming it far too complicated and dangerous, but it was shorter than going north around the Butt of Lewis, or south to Barra Head and offered less open water for the crossing: Cubby knew it well. I had loved every single second since leaving Oban: the space, the swooping, swirling seabirds, the misty blue islands strung out across the soft blue sea, the *whoosh* as the bow cut through the clear rolling swells. Every moment had filled me with a sense of mystery and excitement and even the ceaseless worry of Digby was easing. John's mother knew how to contact the boat, so I fervently hoped no news was good news, but I did wish there had been time to ring and check he was all right.

Squeezing past Kate and Dickie who were chatting in the galley, I knocked on the little door into the wheelhouse. Cubby, at the wheel, had the VHF handset tucked under his chin. He waved me in, still speaking to someone he clearly knew well.

'Thanks, Murdo, it's good to know there's not too much of a swell out there.' The VHF, it seemed, was not just for serious things, but gossip too; not only could you chat, you could also learn about the swell and sea conditions where you were going.

I carefully eased past him and tucked myself into the corner seat out of the way. I looked at the chart – yet another new thing.

'Here you are at last,' he said as if I'd been away for days. 'Could you do a wee job for me? I don't want any others up here while we go through the Sound. But could you tick off each of the damn buoys on the chart as we get on past it? They're that alike it's awful easy to forget where we are.'

'Of course, I'd love to.' I picked up the pencil and peered earnestly at the chart.

'It's not difficult, each has a number. We'll not be in the channel for another hour so you can relax just now.' I stared up at the radar screen above my head. I wondered if that was the land glowing green and the sea that seemed to be black. Cubby rolled another cigarette and occasionally gave the wheel a slight turn; the VHF let out intermittent crackles. In the low afternoon sunlight, fulmars trailed their wing tips through the tops of the waves, slipping sideways through the air overtaking the boat. We sat in companionable silence.

A green blob appeared on the radar. Through my binoculars, I could see a red-and-white buoy far ahead. 'Is that the first buoy?' I asked, hopefully.

'You've sharp eyes,' he said, smiling at me. 'No. That's to mark the entrance to the channel, it's those around the corner you'll need to look out for.'

Once we were past the buoy, he turned the wheel and *Conochbar* headed straight into the sun. Silhouetted in the golden light, I could see the first of the huge channel markers ahead: No. 1. The bell, hanging inside the metal cage, tolled eerily in the gentle motion. Carefully, anxious not to get muddled, I ticked them off one after one as the boat made her way further west. After three hours of weaving through them, the *Conochbar* began to lift in the swell of the open Atlantic and way ahead I could see a small grey smudge just visible on the horizon.

'Is that it? Is that St Kilda?' I asked excitedly. 'Not too far to go then. When do you think we'll get there, Cubby?'

He turned, fixing me with his piercing blue eyes, and grinned. 'Aye, it's deceptive,' he said. 'We'll not be there for about five hours. It's that big it looks near but there's forty miles of open sea to deal with first. You're welcome to stay up here and keep me company.'

We rolled on gently through the night until at last the *Conochbar* was anchored in Village Bay: we'd arrived at St Kilda.

David Livesey was a large man in every sense, over six-foot-tall with a booming laugh, powerful presence and impressive appetite. He and my father had been friends for years but now, the viscount and judge paced the deck like caged lions: they'd been confined on board for long enough. Everyone was on the deck impatiently studying the bay in the clear morning light. The bright green turf and little houses looked enticing and I remembered Coleridge's Ancient Mariner: it was true; you could 'smell land'. Odours of damp earth, sphagnum moss and sheep wafted across the still water.

'Now then,' began Cubby, from his commanding position on top of the wheelhouse. 'Just a wee word before you go ashore.' Pausing for maximum effect, he bent down to unleash the tender, a large grey Zodiac. 'It's the forty-ninth time I've been here and I'm not trusting the place just yet: it's wild and I don't miss a forecast out here. You're to keep your ears open and if you hear the horn you're to come back to the quay. No messing around. I'll be needing you all on board. Fast! No going near cliff edges. No wandering off, and you'll be needing to make your peace with the warden first.'

Kate stuck her head out of the galley window and called along the deck to us, 'Will ye be taking a piece in a poke?'

'Yes please, that would be lovely, thank you,' responded Dickie at once. I wondered what was going on now and why every comment seemed laced with *double entendres*. Paper bags appeared stuffed with sandwiches – a piece in a poke, another thing learnt.

Like razorbills along a ledge, we sat on the tubes of the Zodiac while Cubby drove us across the bay towards the small stone quay. The steps disappeared into the depths, easily visible in clear water. Seaweed swooshed up and down, back and forth in the slight swell, the fronds of the deep brown bladderwrack waved like trees in a gale. Gingerly we helped each other up the slippery steps. My legs didn't really feel under control; I had already acquired 'sea legs' from the hours on board and I wobbled up onto the quay top, gazing round in awe, silenced by the massive encircling sweep of the bay. Wafts of sheep shit, stronger now and tinged with beer, brushed aside any sense of romance. Kittiwakes shrieked from the cliffs and puffins bobbed around the Zodiac like self-important waiters hoping for a tip.

The peace was shattered by Veronica's cut-glass tones. 'Damn, I'm stuck. Darling! *Do* help! Don't just stand there *gawping*! Come here!' One of her high heels was wedged between the stones of the quay. Caught in a crack, she was rooted to the spot and unable to move. A man clad in regulation Nature Conservancy green bounded down the slope towards us, staring incredulously at the figure, resplendent in black leopard-print jeans, stilettoes and the ever-present Hermes scarf, stuck at the top of the quay.

He stopped in amazement as Vernon spread out his mac like Walter Raleigh. He knelt down, easing her heel out of the crack while Veronica swayed, standing on the mac on one foot, precariously close to the quay edge.

Nick was the keen-as-mustard warden, in his second summer working for the nature conservancy on Hirta, the main island of the St Kilda archipelago. He had obviously been primed as to who was coming and the purpose behind our visit. He pulled off his bobble hat, stretching out a hand. 'Hello! So glad you've made it! Where's the *vissss*count?' he asked courteously. 'Is he still on the *Conochbar*?'

'No, I'm here, thank you,' David replied, holding out his hand.

'I do hope the crossing wasn't too rough, sir. The weather's been great here the last few days and the forecast's good too, so you should be able to have some great walks, right out to the far end of Hirta if you want to, sir,' he enthused. 'But please keep away from the cliff edges. I don't want you slipping over, sir. There's no one out here to rescue you, you know. And you must watch out if you're up on the top for the skuas. They're nesting at the moment and they're pretty aggressive, sir. It's best to wear a hat up there cos they'll dive-bomb you if you get close to a nest. They can make a nasty gash in your head.' I wondered if St Kilda had inspired Daphne du Maurier.

We strolled, stretching our cramped legs, towards what had once been the village. The tight, short turf was bouncy and spattered everywhere with gobbets of sheep shit and tufts of chocolate brown wool. Tiny cottages, stretched out like a string of white pearls echoing the curve of the bay, all faced out to sea, turning their window-less backs to the bleak slopes of the island's peaks. Some of the diminutive stone buildings had ropes crossing over the top with stones tied on the ends to prevent the turf roof being blown away by the wind, but most were simply open to the sky. Each had once been a family's home and each had a slate propped up by the door, nestling amongst the nettles, with the family's name. One or two had been reroofed and were used by the National Trust for their volunteers who came each summer to do archaeological work. One had been turned into a simple museum and one by one we ducked through the low stone doorway into the dim cool interior. Black-and-white photographs hung round the tiny room with its sturdy stone walls. Swarthy, warmly clad women sat solidly amongst mounds of seabird feathers, while the men, dressed in Sunday suits, posed, hands clutching bunches of dead sea birds, gazing steadily at the camera. The extraordinary life of the islanders, in all its isolation and harshness, came echoing out of the photos.

The following days were filled with exploring. We picnicked on the dense turf close to the cliff edges, watched whales and marvelled at the squabbling black guillemots and razorbills packed onto the ledges of the sheer cliffs. None of us paid much attention to Cubby's pronouncements about how lucky we were, how the weather was not usually so settled and how rarely his passengers were free to come and go across the bay. About thirty people lived on Hirta during the summer – the National Trust volunteers and a Signals Regiment detachment. They whiled away the long light evenings playing pub games at the Puff-Inn enlivened by the double measures and offshore prices. It was breathtakingly magical but through it all ran a thread of anxiety. Digby. I kept wondering how he was but there was no means of finding out as communications out here were only for emergencies.

After four glorious days the anchor chain came clanking on board. Now as we studied the village, it seemed different, lonely and desolate. Kate leant over the side pointing to where the chain emerged from the clear water while Cubby steered in the direction she pointed. No need to wash off any mud, the bottom of Village Bay was sandy and clean. *Conochbar* turned her stern to the sweep of the bay and started nosing out into the open sea. The deck began to lift gently in the slight swell and already the village and pub were slipping away astern. Turning to starboard, we headed

27

south-west, out around the rocky crags of Dun to weave a course through the huge stacs of the outer fringes of the archipelago. The afternoon sun was warm and even Veronica, feet clad in Vernon's socks, was out on deck with her binoculars and camera. Cubby had threatened to hurl her high heels over the side if they appeared again on deck.

The grandeur was overpowering; the cliffs and walls of rock rose hundreds of feet straight up out of the sea so that it was difficult to grasp a sense of scale. Scattered across the steep slopes of the next island, Boreray, were tiny brown dots. One moved: a sheep. Dwarfed by the vastness of the cliffs, they grazed unconcerned by the sheer drop below. What looked like an explosion of feathers drifting in the wind turned out to be gannets flying to and fro from the packed and smelly colonies on the tooth-like stacs of Lee and An Armin. I looked back at the island of Hirta where we had strolled and picnicked in the sun. I thought of the harsh life the villagers had led; with no trees their boat had been made of driftwood and was too precious to use for fishing. They had survived on dried sea birds and eggs collected from the cliffs and had paid their rent to the Lord of the Isles in feathers and sea bird oil.

The *Conochbar* dipped and rolled her way back east towards the Outer Hebrides, across the open Atlantic, but the night passed quickly. I kept Cubby company in the tiny wheelhouse, and early the next morning we were at the entrance to the Sound of Harris. Again, it was fun to do what I now regarded as 'my' job, ticking off the buoys marking the channel as we carried on south-east. This time there was no leg-stretching on North Uist, and the following afternoon as the sun dropped towards the horizon behind us we reached Canna, one of the Small Isles. Protected by Rum, Eigg and Muck, Canna, Cubby told me, was the most luxuriant: a volcanic island, anchored in the middle of the prawn-rich fishing grounds of the Minch and for him a regular stop. Its only farm produced the best Golden Wonder potatoes in the world, he insisted, and he never missed an opportunity to stock up. After the barren bones of the treeless Hebrides, the little pockets of dense woodland and tiny meadows welcomed us, and we could hear birdsong and a cow mooing. It seemed like a garden.

David Livesey's friend Sir John Lorne Campbell, who owned the island, had invited us to dinner.

'So you're off to the big house?' Cubby remarked, pointing to a neat granite building which peered out over bright fuchsia hedges as our boat settled to swing gently at anchor in the sheltered harbour. I was longing to meet this man who had planted trees and changed the island so much, but perhaps even more, to meet his wife. David had said she had been present at the evacuation of St Kilda, when the villagers had finally chosen to leave their homes and island life in 1930. With most of their menfolk killed in the Great War, life on Hirta had become barely tenable and they had asked to be evacuated. Little had they known how insensitively the evacuation would be handled. They had been made to kill their own dogs and cats: no pets were allowed to go with them; families were split up and the men, most of whom had never seen a tree in their lives, were sent to work for the Forestry Commission. Lady Campbell must have quite a story to tell.

Cubby nosed the Zodiac onto the sand with his cargo of scrubbed up passengers – my mother in regulation tweed skirt, the men wearing ties and Veronica, high heels in hand, was resplendent in black velvet trousers whilst I was in a summery dress. It was blissfully warm after the chilly winds of the sea and we strolled slowly up the little drive, the air thick with the heady scent of meadowsweet. Purple spotted orchids poked up through the short grass and bees buzzed amongst the sprays of dog roses. Inside, the house was cool with the chill typical of a thick-walled northern house in summer. It was warmer out than in. I shivered as I followed my mother into the drawing room. Through the open window I could see Cubby, like a water boatman beetle, rowing slowly back to the *Conochbar:* he hated the noise of the outboard motor and rowing was good exercise.

Dinner was encouragingly hot and completely delicious: roast venison with, of course, those Golden Wonder potatoes, followed by wild raspberries and thick cream. Not a hint of a banana yoghurt. Nor was there a phone. I was longing to ring John's mother and hear how the boys were, but Cubby's VHF blethering about potatoes and fish had already established that the island's only telephone, a call box tucked into the wall by the little kirk, was out of action.

When Sir John had bought the island there was not a tree anywhere, but he had a keen interest in Hebridean butterflies and had planted copses and woodlands with purely indigenous species: the butterflies and moths had arrived. His collection rested in a Victorian butterfly cabinet and after dinner he pulled out drawer after slim drawer from the tall mahogany cabinet, each of the specimens was meticulously displayed and labelled. Butterflies and moths glowed, gold and yellow, frail wings and dainty curled antennae; each was impaled by a thick pin straight through its tiny furry body.

Disappointingly, his frail wife seemed to remember little of the evacuation and was unwilling to talk about it, in spite of Veronica's journalistic prompting, but she was an ardent collector of the Gaelic folksongs peculiar to the Hebrides. After dinner, sitting silhouetted against the silver waters of bay, she sang in a soft, lilting voice, crooning Gaelic love songs to the reedy accompaniment of a harpsichord. Quietly, I eased myself away from the party. In the hall the damp cool air of the big stone house closed round me as I tiptoed carefully to the front door. Turning the smooth brass doorknob, I slipped out into the soft twilight. No one had noticed me go.

Outside in the garden it was warm and welcoming, fragrant with cut grass and roses. I shook off the oppressive musty gloom, the haunting songs and visions of the impaled bodies of butterflies, and made my way across the soft lawn towards the gate in the fuchsia hedge.

'It's yourself!' I jumped as Cubby detached himself from the deep shadows of the hedge: his arm snaked round my waist and he brushed the lightest kiss at the side of my lips. We strolled down the drive, deep in shadow from the summer leaves to the harbour and sat on the wall, still warm from the afternoon sun, to wait for the others.

Three

It was an idyllic introduction but it was thanks to John that our series of family voyages began. I had 'sprung' Diggers from Great Ormond Street Hospital. He had clung on to me like a limpet, grinning from ear to ear. The hospital gurus, unable to work out what was wrong, were consistently insensitive and seemed to think he was both deaf and stupid. He loathed being talked 'about' and after three weeks of what he felt was prison, I had to get him home, out of the hot rooms that drained him and back to food that suited his confused digestion. He still couldn't walk, but he could sing in an angelic, pure choirboy's voice. He was also charmingly wicked and the two boys worked as a team, swapping price tags in supermarkets and moving things around on the shelves. He loved animals, had a pet rabbit and would be angry with John when he went shooting. He could ride a horse, and chatted ceaselessly, full of jokes and fun. But no one knew why he was so frail, why he regularly caught pneumonia, or why he couldn't walk, why he overheated and why his skin would rub off like a massive burn. It was clear he was in pain much of the time and at night was rarely peaceful or asleep. Making his life manageable absorbed me day and night. I thought of little else, expending most of my energy devising strategies to help him, to entertain and divert him. But in amongst the horrors and frights of daily life, he was fantastic fun. Hugo, fit, strong and three years older, adored him. The brothers were simply inseparable.

As I carried him down the hospital steps, there they were, John and Hugo, waiting for us together with Conker, our unruly springer spaniel. Finally, we were on our way home, to a proper supper. Sitting in the kitchen, tea was celebratory fish fingers and frozen peas with pools of ketchup, Diggers' choice. John looked round the table.

'Diggers, are you feeling like an adventure? Dickie and I have booked a boat for us all to have a holiday at sea. What do you think, you two? Would you like that?' I stared at John in amazement. Over the past years, since we had first gone to St Kilda with my father's party, I had been up to crew for Kate and Cubby on several occasions. The boys knew all about the boat, Digby had even written a poem about it and of course he knew Dickie who had delivered him, but it had always been a 'grown-ups' thing.'

Four months after our initial St Kilda trip, my involve-ment as crew had started with the phone insistently trilling across the lawn where the boys rolled about inside a tepee of bamboo sticks and drying-up cloths. I ran into the kitchen.

'Hello?' Silence. 'Hello!' I bellowed, annoyed at being interrupted. Click, loud breathing.

'Is it yourself?'

Cubby. No one else had that rich sexy voice.

'Hello – what a surprise! Shall I ring you back?'

There were rattling noises as money was pushed into the payphone box. 'Aye, if you don't mind.' He gave me the number: Glasgow. Whatever could he be doing there?

'It's so good to hear you. How are you? Are you in Glasgow?' Until he gave me the number I had visualised him leaning against the side of a lone phone box in a little white village tucked into the shore of a distant sea loch, miles away in the Highlands, wind-buffeted and lit with sparkling reflections off the waves.

'Aye, well, we're away down south, on the Clyde.' This was really unexpected; I'd never imagined him being anywhere so industrial. 'The boat's been up the slip and she's just about finished now. She'll be back in the water in a couple of days, then it'll be round the Mull wi' the tide and back to Oban. Would you fancy coming up for the ride?'

Thus began the first of my trips on board the *Conochbar* as crew. John had been supportive, recognising that I needed breaks from the continuous strain of keeping Digby alive, and Sarah, our wonderful helper, together with a stalwart pair of grannies, had managed during the times I had been away.

I could not have been more nervous at the start. I had never flown anywhere by myself, or done much on my own at all. I had met John when I was sixteen and we'd got married when I was nineteen. He'd been my first and only boyfriend, so venturing off by myself had seemed both grown-up and daunting.

The descending plane swooped over a wide river and I peered out of the window: this must be the Clyde. Red and green marks stretched along the water, which I supposed must be buoys marking the shipping channel. A white bridge curved smoothly over the river while matchbox-sized cars whizzed across it and toy boats slid underneath.

'Ladies and gentlemen, welcome to the European City of Culture.' There was a collective gasp of surprise. The air hostess continued smoothly, 'The time in Glasgow is 14.35 and this year, Glasgow is the European City of Culture!'

Already it felt 'foreign' and far more exciting than arriving by train as I had earlier that summer with my parents.

Not wanting to arrive at the boat empty-handed, I bagged a carton of wine, a flashy-looking box of chocolates and a couple of magazines as I left the airport and leapt into the first available taxi. I hoped Cubby's rather vague directions would make sense to the driver.

'I'd like to go to Gareloch, please, to a shipyard called Timbercraft. It's just next to the submarine base at Faslane.' The taxi driver didn't bat an eyelid. Fusty with cigarette smoke and stale beer, the car climbed out of the airport, struggling up the slip road and onto the M8. Over the bridge I'd seen from the air the taxi lumbered and I paid the toll while the driver grumbled about the cost. Turning into the sun, I concluded we were driving west along the north bank of the Clyde.

Prim Victorian houses appeared – *Helensburgh*, the sign told me. The neat Victorian villas had blue hydrangea bushes billowing over solid garden walls, and they gazed smugly across the still water while dainty yachts swung on moorings. Abruptly this suburban idyll was interrupted by a stern ten-foot-high chain-link fence. A man with a machine gun glared out from behind the fence. *Keep Out*, shouted a sign, in big red letters. Looming through the fence was a mountainous black hulk: more men were spaced at regular intervals along the top of the black hulk, their machine guns silhouetted by the silver waters of the loch. A nuclear sub. Huge and menacing, it made a startling contrast to the gentle hills and peaceful surroundings.

'Is this it?' I asked incredulously.

'Aye,' was the terse reply. I levered myself out of the sunken back seat, clutching the goodies and box of wine, wondering what to do next. Dumped in the empty road I watched the taxi slowly disappear, conscious of the guns and sub just over my shoulder; I turned to study it through the chain-link fencing.

'Hi there! You've made it!' Kate's powerful Glaswegian voice bellowed out behind me: I jumped and dropped the box of wine.

'Oh! Hello! It's so nice to be here! How are you?' I gushed nervously. She scooped up my bag as I grabbed the booze and chocolates and followed her down the side of the unyielding fence along a well-worn track leading down to the shore of the loch. It seemed curious just to walk into the open again to find a huge shed with one end exposed to the waters of the loch. Inside the shed, pulled up high out of the water, was a very shiny *Conochbar*, so much smarter than I remembered. Her superstructure glowed, a freshly painted shiny white even in the gloom of the shed, and the hull glistened with crisp black paint, whilst her bottom was a deep brick-red with new antifouling. Separating the black from the red was a neat white line running horizontally around the hull. Cubby appeared, coming swiftly down the ladder onto the concrete, clad as ever in yellow oilskins and wellies.

'Hullo. You're here at last.' His bright 'sea' eyes fixed me with a steady gaze. I remembered noticing the fishermen I'd met en route to St Kilda all had a most penetrating look — maybe all that staring into the far distance. He gave me a welcoming kiss.

The invitation to join them had been a surprise. English, from a privileged background and with no experience of the sea, I had been offered this beautiful coastal voyage. To travel down the Gareloch into the Clyde, round the treacherous Mull of Kintyre through the North Channel, then to weave through the island chains of Islay and Jura, past Crinan and Kerrera and eventually to Oban, was a voyage to relish. Three days of sensational scenery and carefree existence. I'd looked at the map and knew exactly how lucky I was.

'Flight OK?' he asked. 'Do you like the boot top?'

'I didn't know your wellies were so important!' I replied, surprised.

'Get away!' he laughed. 'It's the white line on the hull. It may be a wee bit fancy for a fishing boat, but I like it. It looks smart and it's the first time she's had one. I've made them paint it a bit wider at the bow, a wee bit narrower mid-ships and then again wider at the stern. It'll give her length. Aye, and slim her down too, make her less of a fishing boat,' he said proudly. Then, taking all my things in one hand, he effortlessly climbed the ladder using the other. Constant clambering up and down ladders was a skill I needed to learn and quickly, I realised; they were usually the only way on or off. Bolted up the side of a quay, they became a vertical slippery challenge and at low water they were even longer with the bottom section, revealed by the low tide, frequently festooned with slithery seaweed. Some had fixings missing and swayed unnervingly against the quay; some had broken rungs and big gaps. Sometimes there'd be a bar in the quay top to grab onto, otherwise it was best to kneel in the inevitable puddle and get away from the edge before standing up. I learnt I had to embrace them all and be quick at climbing them, ready at the top to catch a rope.

Kate chatted away, asking me about the flight. How were John, my parents – she remembered them all. Cubby asked about Diggers and Hugo, which was touching, as he'd never met them. Then he added, 'And will you be taking a wee sensation?'

'I've a cake somewhere in that bag,' I volunteered wondering about the 'sensation', then was afraid this might be treading on Kate's toes, although home-made cakes had not appeared at any time during our voyage.

'Here's your wee sensation!' he went on, handing me a generous dram.

'And,' I carried on triumphantly, 'a box of wine.' Released from the plastic carrier bag it dripped steadily onto the carpet. 'Oh no, it's sprung a leak!' I wailed. 'What shall we do? Shall we decant it?'

'No, no, we'll just have to drink like fuck!' Cubby growled, grinning.

Next morning a party of divers arrived: five burly policemen from Burnley, who knew Kate and Cubby from their previous dive trips. Unlike me, who was fascinated to see the hull exposed and completely out of the water, they were familiar with it all. Dive suits on coat hangers and heavy bags with *Scubapro* in big yellow letters along the sides were loaded on board, Cubby reminding them in a no-nonsense voice where to stow everything.

Thud! Thud! Thud! Conochbar shook throughout her whole length: the thuds came increasingly loudly from under the hull. Peering over the side, I could see men lobbing huge hammers to loosen the wedges holding her onto the wooden carriage. Cubby was quickly on deck. 'Keep Away! Stand back! Don't get near the gunwales!' He bellowed and ran light-footed through the galley back into the wheelhouse. Creaking slightly, the carriage, *Conochbar* and all on board crept slowly but steadily backwards out of the shed towards the calm waters of the loch. The concrete slipway fifteen feet below slipped underneath faster and faster. Gaining speed, her weight took her in an unstoppable rush backwards into the sea.

Whoosh! Her stern dug deep into the water, pushing the sea aside. For a moment she hesitated, rolled from side to side, and then calmly bobbed up like a bath toy, at home again, a boat in her element. Cubby's dire tales the previous evening about snapping ropes and unchecked rushes into the water were unfounded. All was fine: she hadn't fallen over and nothing had broken loose, because he had of course made sure everything was secure. Wavelets spread out, rippling the reflections of trees, hills and little houses strung along the shore as we bobbed on the still waters of the Gareloch in the morning sunshine. After a moment the engine, a green Gardner much admired for its reliability by Cubby, throbbed into life, and Kate up in the wheelhouse turned the *Conochbar* south, heading towards the open waters of the Clyde. Standing on deck, I couldn't resist giving a wave to the security guard looking down from the sub and he coolly lifted a hand from his gun and saluted. It was a most perfect peaceful morning.

Cubby appeared, oily from the engine room, having checked all was tidy, neatly stowed and to hand if needed. Soon we'd be out of the Clyde and the passage round the Mull of Kintyre was not to be taken lightly. When a boat left a shipyard, he'd told me, you could never be sure some careless worker hadn't left a rag lying about ready to slip into the bilges and block a pump, or there might even be a sea cock left open to flood the hull. He was deeply sceptical of everyone else's concern for safety; in his eyes no one was as careful as he was, not even Kate. Having checked the engine room meticulously, he went to relieve Kate. Hoping to be inconspicuous, and very conscious of my Home Counties accent, I went up to the wheelhouse and tucked myself on the seat at the port side by the window. The divers were clearly at home flirting with Kate. The loch stretched ahead as bracken-clad shores and yachts, lazing on moorings, slid past. Cubby occasionally turned the wheel, a smell of frying bacon drifted up towards us out of the galley, and all was calm in the beautiful morning sunshine, just the VHF chattering away as Clyde Coastguard spoke to yachts. Cubby picked up the handset, waiting for a break and then pressed the button:

'Clyde Coastguard, Clyde Coastguard, this is *Conochbar*, *Conochbar*.'

'*Conochbar*, this is Clyde Coastguard, channel 67.'

'67.'

Stretching backwards, he leant towards the green VHF Sailor radio on the wall behind him. 'Clyde Coastguard, this is *Conochbar*. Good morning to you. We're heading round the Mull for Oban. Nine people on board. Thanks for your help and we'll speak again when we're next on the Clyde.' It was fun to be back and ensconced in the wheelhouse: I wondered if there would be any buoys for me to tick off the chart this time. *Conochbar* began to lift gently as we made our way south, out past Bute towards Ailsa Craig.

'OK, it's your turn now. Just keep her on 220°. I've a few things to check on deck. Keep an eye on the oil pressure and give a shout if it changes.' Before I had time to speak he'd gone, and I was alone in the wheelhouse. Gingerly, I turned the wheel just a little bit, to see what it felt like. Quickly she was angled towards the shore; I turned the wheel back. Too far. Now the opposite shore was straight ahead. Take it gently, I said to myself, just little movements. I tried to relax and hummed a little tune in the hope of convincing myself. I knew he'd be keeping an eye out while coiling the ropes and stowing the fenders as he chatting with the divers, who seemed to be huddled over a small black box. I hummed a bit more, looking around, checking for other boats, trying to feel in charge.

Suddenly, the *Conochbar* began to lift up, and up: she sped forwards, coursing down a wave like a surfer. I looked wildly from side to side as the whole wheelhouse was engulfed in shadow and the starboard window went black as a sub blotted out the light. We were lifted up like a toy, as the huge machine pushed a mound of water ahead of it, and swept down the loch. Black and menacing it surged on purposefully, evil and threatening. A moment later, I watched as it quietly slid below the water and with barely ripple it was gone; the loch was calm again. I plonked myself down behind the wheel, legs dangling weakly from the high seat and glanced at the compass: still on 220°, I breathed a sigh of relief.

'*Conochbar! Conochbar!* This is *Black Widow, Black Widow.*' I jumped again as the VHF burst out behind me.

'*Conochbar! Conochbar!* This is *Black Widow, Black Widow.*'

'*Conochbar! Conochbar!* This is *Black Widow, Black Widow. Conochbar*, are you receiving me?' The voice became increasingly insistent.

In theory I knew how to reply, but if I did the whole of the west coast would hear and wonder. But it wouldn't do just to ignore the call. Nervously, I picked up the black handset and pressed the transmit button: '*Black Widow! Black Widow!* This is *Conochbar*, channel seven-zero.' I responded, stretching back to twirl the dial, holding my breath.

'Hello there, *Conochbar*! *Black Widow* here. Long

time no see! We noticed you heading down the loch and wondered how you are. What've you been up to?' I scanned the windows, no boat, nothing. Firmly I pressed the button. 'Hello, *Black Widow*. Cubby's out on deck and Kate's in the galley. Can I give one of them a shout for you?' I asked, not wanting to elaborate.

'Well, who are you, then?' they persisted. 'What are you doing on board?'

'Oh, I'm just here for a few days to lend a hand,' I replied, realising it sounded a bit lame. I glanced round again checking there was nothing that needed avoiding. I looked at the compass, 225°: just a little movement needed.

I waited, wondering what would be the response. A faint sound of chuckling drifted through the open window. Standing on the bow, the group of divers waved and giggled, holding up the small black box, its aerial pointing skywards. I grinned and waved back, trying not to mind having been made to look a fool.

Of course I had returned home full of stories, and of course the boys had loved hearing tales of submarines and Mummy being in charge of the boat. So now sitting together with just the crumbs of fish fingers left, they were overcome with excitement at John's suggestion. After the frightening tests, smells and noises of the hospital the open spaces of the sea were a heady prospect.

It was a complete success, so over the next three years we had a succession of wonderful family summer holidays. Other families joined us from time to time, and in between I went up on my own to help cook or to be a deck hand, especially during winter dive charters. With no children of their own, Kate and Cubby had welcomed the boys and they both completely adored Diggers. Life on a boat suited him perfectly. Kate spoilt him with food that was banned at home whilst Cubby would hoist him on his shoulders and go striding off across the bog and heather telling him stories of witches, hobgoblins and elves. We swam in the burns, splashed about in waterfalls and caught wily brown trout in little mountain lochs. Cubby created little expeditions for Diggers and the other children – no adults allowed. He would pile them all in the Zodiac and putter off across the lochs to lay creels baited with the remains of smoked salmon. Pulling up the creels, the boys found bright blue lobsters and deep brown crabs scrabbling around in the bottom. Hugo learnt to windsurf and Diggers, agile when he was on all fours, could clamber in and out of the Zodiac with ease. He thrived in the cool climate and had an unerring sense of balance. He discovered that on a boat people couldn't walk off and leave him behind and, better still, unlike some, he was never sea sick. They were idyllic summer holidays.

Four

Those golden holidays seemed long gone and I couldn't even let myself remember them or I felt I would slip down into a hole, never to climb out. We had left London six months earlier when John had opened a new office for his company in Manchester; we had friends around there and it seemed good to escape London. Hugo was away at boarding school and John split his time between Manchester and London: he would leave home on Monday morning to work in the Manchester office then carry on down to London, not coming back until Friday evening. I was again by myself and unutterably lonely.

Digby's bedroom threatened upstairs, empty, silent but still alive with him. The smell of him. The charm of his giggles. What should I do with his precious collections of seashells and seeds, his clothes, his toys and his books?

Three months earlier, I'd gone into his room to wake him for school. He rarely slept well but he looked angelic, slightly flushed, a gentle snore drifting up from the bed. I decided a day off school for an eight-year-old would do no harm. I went back to the ironing.

Glancing at the kitchen clock a little later, I saw it was 9.30, so I needed to get him up, or he would not sleep at all that night. There was no little sound of gentle snoring as I walked down the passage and as soon as I looked at him I knew. He was completely still and his lips were pale blue.

Over the next few months, life seemed to take place beyond a thick pane of glass. I was an observer, numb with no feelings. Just an all-consuming, aching emptiness. What should I have done? Why had I not gone upstairs sooner? I tried to fill the time. I didn't eat, drink or do anything much. The doctor gave me some pills. One in the morning and one at bedtime, working up to four a day but when I took the first one I'd slept until mid-morning and then was unable to get out of bed or walk to the bathroom. I was too frightened to take any more.

I didn't want to be in the house with all its memories; everywhere I looked was Digby. His clothes. His toys. His pet rabbit. The funny things he'd said rang round my head.

He would never come back. I'd never again feel his bony little body snuggling close. I'd never hear his chuckles. I'd never hear his little songs again. The sweet smell of him.

I seemed to have no purpose in life.

There was no one to break the silence.

No one to talk to. No one to cook for. No one to look after.

Just me. In a house that was no longer a home.

The phone rang. Desperate, I grabbed it.

Clank. Chink. I could hear coins dropping into the box.

46

'Hullo there! It's yourself! How are you keeping? Are you OK?' Cubby's soft west coast voice purred down the line. I took a deep breath, pushing back the tears and tried to put a smile into my voice. Of course they knew about Digby but his query about me was still almost too much.

'Hello. Yes, it's me,' I blurted. 'How are you? It's such an age since I heard from you. How's Kate? Where've you been? Where are you now? Do you want me to call you back?' I rushed on, trying to prevent myself bursting into tears.

'Aye, well, it's been a wee while. It's not been so easy. I'm afraid I've no good news.' Knowing Cubby's dislike of the telephone I wondered why he was ringing. His voice went on, 'I'm sorry but you'll not be able to come up here again.'

'I'll call you back. What's the number?' I said firmly. I knew he was quite capable of just walking away, back to the boat, having said what he needed to say and not wanting to get drawn into more detail.

An hour later, the longest I'd ever spent on the phone to him, he had told me the news. Cubby and Kate were employed to operate the *Conochbar* and Cubby had told me that after running the boat successfully for twelve years, their employment was being brought to an end. It seemed the owner wanted the boat for himself and without the arduous commitment of taking the National Trust volunteers out to St Kilda.

I wandered around the house, trying to assemble my thoughts and get my frozen brain to work. I reckoned there were two choices: turn away or get involved. I knew, right then, sitting alone in the empty house, as I gazed out at sheep dotted about in the fields beyond the garden, I couldn't just ignore their difficulties. They'd become good friends.

But I also knew it might be a turning point in my life.

Two days later, I got out of the house going north on the A74, whizzing past Carlisle and Gretna Green. I had relayed my long call-box discussions with Cubby to John. Decisive as always, he knew they could run a boat and could see the potential from our happy family holidays. I knew he liked the prospect of establishing his own business: it would be his 'retirement job', he said. With his knowledge of the financial world, he would set the business up to offer tax advantages and other incentives. We just needed people to invest, not too much, so that a loss would be unmanageable, but enough so we could buy a boat for Kate and Cubby to run. But he told me I needed to meet the National Trust for Scotland, to persuade them to give us the contract: we must have some predictable income from the outset.

All I had to do was find a boat and acquire the National Trust's St Kilda contract. Simple!

In the Trust's offices in Edinburgh I spelled out our plans. I reminded them we'd be employing Cubby, whom they already knew as reliable, efficient, and above all safe.

'I think it went well,' I said to John seated in the *Flying Tomato*. I had a splendid new state-of-the-art toy – a mobile phone. Sitting beside me on the

48

passenger seat, with its erect little black aerial quivering like a running warthog's tail, it was the size of a small suitcase. Back in 1989 these were early days for mobiles but John, realising I needed to escape from the painful memories of home, had given me a Motorola. I loved it immediately. Not only was it a cutting-edge, stylish thing to have, but I no longer needed to be in the house. I no longer missed my friends or when Hugo called from school: I was released. I clicked the handset back into its cradle and set off towards Oban to tell Kate and Cubby such news as I had.

'We'll have to see what the Trust actually does,' I reported later as we sat in the boat's saloon clutching mugs of tea and ploughing through the chocolate biscuits I'd brought with me.

'Aye, but we've not got time to wait,' was Kate's anxious reply as she dragged on yet another cigarette. 'He says we've to be off the boat in two days' time.' They both looked grey and neither had suggested a dram. Things were too serious. This was their world and had been their home for twelve years. All of their possessions were in the small aft cabin. They had nowhere else to go, no house, nothing of their own. John had told me they might have a claim for unfair dismissal, but even so they would have to leave the *Conochbar*.

'Well, John and I are going to do everything we can.' I tried to sound encouraging. 'And right now I'll go and get us a fish supper. Something to eat'll help.' Jumping up, I grabbed a jacket and clambered over the gunwale onto the boat next door, crossed its deck and was quickly up onto the quay before they had a chance to demur. I was good at ladders by now.

It was late November and Oban was dark and deserted. Fishing boats slumbered three or four deep along the quay, their masts, a tangle of steel struts, glowed orange in the sodium street lights. The chip shop was not far, just across the square past the station. I walked back towards the pier, clutching the bag of fish suppers. It was warm and soft and reminded me of carrying Diggers; most things reminded me of him. Tired and lost in thoughts of his warmth, I didn't see the figure detach itself and come towards me along the quay.

'You get your fancy hi'-falooting self out of here. You're not wanted!'

Startled, I stopped and stared. Then I began to run, just wanting to get away along the pier back to the warmth and safety of the *Conochbar*. In my haste, I slipped and crashed down into a puddle of cold stinking fishy water. Who was it? Never, in my tidy, sheltered life had anything like this happened to me before. I'd never been shouted at, or the butt of such venom. With my nose inches from the slippery concrete, I peered between my knees and caught a glimpse of a figure furtively scurrying off, getting quickly away. Frightened, I knelt in the cold, fishy water, trying to get my breath. Eventually I managed to crawl to the edge of the quay, gasping to find enough breath to shout. 'Cubby! Cubby!' I wheezed. Up he came, jumping over the gunwales, as light as a shadow, up the ladder and onto the quay.

There was no one to be seen, whoever it was; they were well and truly gone, not wanting a fight.

The fish suppers were good but none of us ate much. Next morning, we woke to find the trawlers between us and the quay had slipped away during the night, off to get on with fishing, so that now the *Conachbar* was exposed and easy to board. It was time to get out of Oban. Last night's threat might lead to something worse and we reckoned we knew where it came from. Dispiritedly, we roped Cubby and Kate's belongings up onto the quay, everything they owned, and the three of us squeezed into the *Flying Tomato*. With no prospect of work, they would have little to live on for the coming winter; we set off down the coast to Loch Melfort. Cubby's parents lived in a tiny house next to the pub; they could stay there while John and I worked on the next stages of the plan.

It was Friday and the start of Hugo's half-term, which we had decided to spend amongst the distractions of London. It would be more cheerful for us all, better than the emptiness of home in November, soulless without Diggers. Wearily I began the long drive south to join them. The *Flying Tomato* whizzed down the empty road along the shores of Loch Long, and as ever thoughts of Digby seeped into my mind. But Hugo and John would be waiting. Seven hours later I drew into Park Lane and the pools of crisp light at the entrance to the Intercontinental Hotel. Jumping out, I handed the keys to the liveried doorman who looked down his nose at the small, mud-spattered car.

51

Swinging through the revolving glass door into the bright marble foyer I was aware of a distinct whiff of fish and salt trailing behind me.

Five

After leaving Kate and Cubby jobless and lodged with Cubby's mother, I had trawled through endless yachty magazines, the *Fishing News* and shipping agents' adverts – no Internet or Google then. Even teatime at home with Hugo had become a boat hunt. 'I like this one!' he cried, spotting yet another glossy, white, super-yacht, sleek with sun loungers and awnings. Cubby and I followed up every possibility, scouring the country from Dundee to Devon, zooming around in the *Flying Tomato*, staying in frilly B&Bs, dreary Travelodges and pubs. It was fun and Cubby, loving the changes of scene and new places, was full of curiosity and interest in all the places we visited, so was the perfect driving companion. But the search was also utterly dispiriting and time was running out. Eight months had passed since Kate and Cubby had left the *Conochbar*. It had seemed doable, to find and equip a vessel so we could meet the National Trust charter deadline, but the months had slipped away. John had signed the contract and we were already committed to their schedule of voyages. The first group was to be transported to St Kilda early in May. Financially all was organised, our investors would fund the boat purchase, John had prised a loan and grant out of the Highlands & Islands Development Board and the Clydesdale Bank had agreed a marine mortgage, so all was ready.

But as the date of the first voyage had crept ever nearer, we still had no boat. However, at last a fuzzy photo of a large trawler advertised by a shipping agent in Grimsby had seemed a possibility. 'Yes, no problem,' the agent said. 'Of course you can see her. She's available for inspections. She's at her home port in Denmark.'

Cubby was the key to the venture, and we were completely dependent on his knowledge. Born on the wild west coast island of Jura, when a boy Cubby had helped his father fish the infamous whirlpools of the Corryvreckan, *the cauldron of the speckled seas*. Together they had heaved up creels of scrabbling lobsters for the gentry, pulling up the heavy baskets by hand from the turbulent dark waters into the bouncing rowing boat. But by the age of twelve he had to leave the little island school of Jura for Oban, the big city. It was everything he hated: no more running wild, squirming through the heather and bracken to sneak up on sleeping deer, no more tickling salmon from the laird's lochs. After two grim years of boarding with a prim-faced spinster in Oban he had packed his bags and gone down to the harbour. He had been at sea ever since.

We had quickly learnt there would be no compromise on the kind of boat Cubby wanted. His veins seemed to run with saltwater rather than blood and he trusted fishing boats, knew their strengths and what was needed for working in the turbulent North Atlantic waters beyond the Outer Hebrides. Being responsible for lives at sea had confirmed his inflexible views. To have twelve passengers forty miles out in inhospitable seas beyond the reach of rescue services at inaccessible St Kilda – 'forty miles west of bugger all' – required a tough, reliable vessel. It had to be a boat that would be safe and have its own back-up systems. Cubby had spelled out his conditions. While he was desperate to have work and a boat to drive, he still insisted things should be done his way. Compromise, on such important issues, was not a word he recognised.

Together we had looked at so many, each seeming so promising from its photo. From dainty, delicate yachts to pathetic, plastic, once-loved, greying family day boats, we'd gone over them all. With unflagging optimism we'd checked one after another broken hulk, mouldy with leaves and moss. John decided it would be more cost effective to send Cubby to Denmark as we knew by now, after months of inspecting rotting hulks, there was no point in the expense of a marine surveyor making the initial inspection. Cubby would know immediately if the boat was just another disappointing, unseaworthy, moulding wreck.

'What do you mean you won't go? Why ever not?' John was incredulous. All this effort and money to give Cubby a boat and job and yet the man was saying he wouldn't go! To John, at his desk in a neat, air-conditioned London office, Cubby's conditions seemed extraordinary, but even from a distant Scottish phone box, his insistence was clear.

'I'm not going without Amelia. I need her to look after me. I've not been away from Scotland before.'

John was not pleased – the man was saying he wanted to go abroad with his wife! However, it was too late to go back now and he would join us in Denmark a few days later.

'Och, it just won't do! I'm away to tell him,' Cubby jumped up from the bunk. 'I have to tell him. He's got to ease her in a bit.' He wanted to go up four lurching decks on to the bridge to tell the captain how to handle his ferry. It was early January and Cubby and I were being tossed about in a pastel-green Formica cabin halfway across the North Sea en route to inspect the boat. It was rough, horribly rough, and Cubby, having never experienced the motion and claustrophobia of an overnight car ferry, was not happy below decks in the confined cabin. He wanted to be out in the air where he felt more at home.

The big steel lump thundered on, slicing through the dark. As it crashed deep into the troughs between the waves, the whole vessel shook, juddering with the lumbering weight and sheer force of speed. Cubby had never crossed any sea before without being in charge, nor had he had ever been south of Glasgow. Just getting him a passport at the tiny village post office in Loch Melfort had amazed him and caused a stir of excitement.

But now we were on our way; I was taking him Abroad, to Foreign Parts and as it turned out, he loved the novelty of it all. Strapped below on the car deck was the trusty *Flying Tomato* waiting for our arrival into Hamburg from where we would drive north to a Danish ferry port named Søndeborg where our possible boat was for sale.

Cubby persisted: 'It's not safe down here. Come on. Let's away up.' I rather agreed. The juddering felt really frightening and I thought of the oil rigs scattered across this shallow sea dotting the ferry's path. Clinging to the handrails, we staggered up the brightly lit, shiny stairwell. The motion became more and more violent as we fought our way upwards, closer towards the bridge, but thankfully Cubby, pausing to stare out of the windows, became fascinated by the gas flares and clusters of lights from the rather too close oil rigs. He pointed out the red-and-green navigation lights of each safety boat as it heaved up and down in the swells, keeping station near its appointed rig.

Eventually the ferry had slowed down and now in the calm of the River Elbe she cruised into Hamburg in the dark, a crack of dawn glimmering to port. The brightly lit dockyards and the spider's web of cranes lifting containers onto the decks of the densely packed freighters intrigued Cubby; another new sight for him.

The *Flying Tomato* slithered down the car ramp, depositing us on an unknown dock in the middle of Hamburg. Several inches of snow covered the cobbles; it was slippery and still virtually dark. I stared round, anxious not to be skidding down the 'wrong' side of the road. Cubby was not a map reader – charts were different – no satnavs then, but eventually we found our way, gingerly negotiating a maze of sleepy suburbs to head north for Søndeborg along the windswept shores of the Baltic. The sky was leaden and oppressive. Everything was colourless, flat and still, squashed by the weight of the cold. No birds, no movement from the neat little red roofed houses, not a sign of life anywhere. As dawn slowly opened up, the harsh white light reflected off the snow giving way to a thin, wintery daylight. Leaving the snow behind, the snug little *Flying Tomato* ate up the miles while Cubby snoozed peacefully. I pressed on.

Swooping over a bridge several hours later, we had a view of the small harbour below: there was a ferry alongside the quay and neat warehouses lining the harbour. Søndeborg. Maybe there would be just enough light to find the unknown boat mysteriously named *Monaco*. We might just have time. In an hour John and our potential investor, Ian, were due at the little airport.

The harbour was thick with trawlers tied up alongside every quay and jetty, two or three deep. Each looked exactly the same as the next. The same shape and the same colour: all a uniform pale sky blue, with a red waterline and white superstructure. I stopped the car on the edge of a quay and peered through the windscreen, wondering how to find her. Cubby, aroused by the whiff of fish, opened his eyes, tapped his tobacco tin and gazed round: 'Aye, that'll be her, just there.' Even in the fading light, with just a sweeping glance round the harbour, he could pick her out. I turned the *Flying Tomato* along the quay and stopped just at the edge so the headlights could light her up. Fishing a torch from under my seat, I jumped out, but my legs skidded straight from under me. Slithering inelegantly across the cobbles on my bum, I came to a stop with my legs dangling out over the edge of the quay, above the boat. Everything was covered in a clear film of solid ice. Cubby stood happily rolling a cigarette, entirely at home on slippery surfaces, 'Are your legs no longer working?' he enquired, grinning.

Lit by the car headlights, she could be seen quite clearly, the white superstructure and dark windows of the wheelhouse staring out blankly. Under them, stretching across the whole width of the wheelhouse were big red letters, **MONACO**.

It had seemed a curious name from the start, and not at all Danish, but for passengers on the west coast of Scotland it would be unusual and smart: just what I wanted. As I took her in, a movement on the deck caught my eye; Cubby was already on board, tucked down at the side of the deck. Kneeling under the bulwark just by the frames, he was stabbing at the wooden deck with his horn-handled fisherman's knife. Purposefully he jabbed at the planking, trying to dig the steel blade into the wood; I slid carefully over the gunwale and stood beside him, holding my breath.

During our many fruitless drives, I'd listened to endless lectures on different woods for decks and hulls, on rot and worms. The effects of worms, types of worms, thin worms, fat and burrowing worms. I'd learnt about sun on deck timbers, suitable timbers for frames and decks, timbers for planking, about caulking and hanging knees. Now, standing there as the headlights threw deep shadows across the deck, I wondered if we'd come on another wild goose chase.

He looked up, stony faced, before allowing a smile to creep across his face. 'Aye, aye,' he grinned. 'She's fresh! Let's be going.'

'Fresh' I knew was a top compliment. His knife hadn't sunk into the planking; the deck at least was not soft and rotten. Tomorrow we'd get a proper look at her but so far it was encouraging. A little knot of excitement tightened in my stomach as we headed for the airport to meet John and Ian.

While we waited for their plane, we grinned at each other. The knot tightened further as the warmth of the terminal seeped into me. Relieved, I wilted on the plastic bench, drained from the cold, the sleepless ferry crossing and the drive from Hamburg. All around happy families chattered and squabbled as they awaited the plane from Copenhagen bringing Dad home to little Søndeborg for the weekend. Suddenly the whole airport was plunged into the pitch blackness of a power cut. No café lights, no blue computer screens, just a distant faint glow from the runway lights and a dark stunned silence in the Terminal. Somewhere in the little hall a sheep started *baa*-ing loudly and urgently. *Baa! Baa! Baa!* It grew more and more insistent. Lighting was restored, the power cut over, lights flickered back on, bathing red plastic seats and waiting families in a bright, harsh glare. Everyone looked about, staring around. Where was it? Officials scurried around; parents and children looked under benches. There was pandemonium while everyone searched for the sheep – a sheep loose at the airport. We'd all heard it. Where was it? I glanced at Cubby as he watched the bustling officials. His lips twitched under his neat moustache and I remembered his stories of his life on Jura, mimicking gulls, cows and sheep.

Into the chaos strolled a calm, city-suited John, accompanied by a tall gangling man in a grubby anorak. Synthetic fur crept along the hood: this must be Ian. I knew he was a major investor and one of our esteemed directors brought in when John had set up the company. Having taken a number of trips with Kate and Cubby while they ran the *Conochbar*, he'd mentioned he would be interested in any future venture Cubby might be involved with, so here he was. John and Ian had met for the first time a few hours earlier at check-in for the flight. I'd given each of them a copy of the *Fishing News*. It seemed a more appropriate way of identifying a shareholder involved with a decommissioned fishing trawler than a red carnation.

'We've found her!' I couldn't help blurting out. 'We've been on board and Cubby thinks she might be OK – well, the deck's OK at least,' I gabbled, stretching up to kiss John.

'That's good, but you must have driven really fast from Hamburg to get here in the light,' he observed. He was good a puncturing a bubble: we'd only had a moment on the deck and there was everything else, the engine, hydraulics, machinery – the whole boat to learn about.

Cubby had insisted on a room next door to ours, saying he'd get lost in the fancy hotel, but he appeared, neat in clean jeans and navy polo neck, having perfectly well found the bar. John, happy to be out of a suit, was also in jeans, but Ian had not bothered to change.

Dinner, with inevitable herrings, to Cubby's delight, had been excellent and we were a cheerful, if curious little party, happily building our virtual boating empire.

In the morning the roads were still sheeted in ice as I inched the *Flying Tomato* slowly along the quay, this time stopping well back from the edge. A man waved from the wheelhouse and we carefully climbed down the ladder. *Monaco*'s owner, a large friendly Dane, waved his arms about and made rumbling noises which, as none of us spoke Danish, we took to mean he'd start up the engine – we were being offered a sea trial.

Off we went, with the engine throbbing away, *Monaco* moving out of the Søndeborg harbour in the cool winter sunlight. We stood about trying to appear professional, as if sea trials and ship inspections were second nature. Cubby, the only person who knew anything about what we were doing, was nowhere to be seen.

The *Monaco* was an unglamorous, sturdy, industrial side-trawler, built in 1970 entirely of European oak. She was 25 metres long with a draft of 4.8 metres and, as I had learnt, was typically Danish. 'If you've seen one, you've seen 'em all,' I'd been told by the agent in Hull. The only difference was size, and *Monaco* was one of the biggest in the harbour. She was not pretty, hardly romantic and she seemed huge and with curious fishing equipment. Cubby liked her and dismissed the fishing gear as irrelevant. What appealed to him was the way she 'met' the swell and of course her size. Our friendly Dane, sensing a sale, turned her round to head back. The brief sea trial had gone well. Cubby had spent most of the time grubbing about below decks with a torch, prodding his knife into assorted timbers, poking round in the bilges and studying the engine. He was filthy but full of bounce and had a twinkle in his deep blue eyes. He was always full of charm and wit when things were going his way.

John, Ian and I stood about rather awkwardly watching the bustling harbour. A ferry gave three blasts on its whistle as it began to go astern. *Monaco* began to slow down and gently drifted to a halt. With her superstructure acting like a sail in the light winter wind she began to drift straight into the path of the reversing ferry. I glanced up at the wheelhouse: our Danish skipper was staring open-mouthed at the ferry.

'Amelia! Come with me,' Cubby shouted. I ran after him along the deck, following as he ducked into a small opening on the port side where I could hear the engine. The metal floor was slippery with oil, but by now only the top of his head was visible as he disappeared down the ladder towards the engine. I turned, kneeling on the slippery steel plating at the top of the ladder and carefully felt below me for the top rung. Cubby stood by the thumping red engine and put his mouth next to my ear to shout over the noise: 'I reckon it's the gears. He's no clue, yon man up there.' It had taken Cubby barely a moment to form an unfavourable opinion of the Dane's abilities.

'D'you see that?' He pointed to skeleton wheel about a foot in diameter. 'Can you turn yon wheel while I push her back into gear?' Grasping the wheel I waited while he listened, judging the revs for the right moment. As he nodded, I heaved on the wheel. It was stiff but I managed to turn it as he pushed a red lever sticking up through the plating of engine room floor.

There was no crunching of machinery; he'd caught the right moment and the tone of the engine changed to a purposeful beat. I stepped out of his way as he hurtled past me, up the ladder, out on deck. Scrambling up, I followed him. It had only taken a couple of minutes and *Monaco* was still in the ferry's path. Cubby's tousled head appeared from the wheelhouse window. 'Grab a fender, girl!' was the curt instruction. Clearly our mighty Dane had let Cubby take charge and there was just time for me to lob a big orange fender over the side. Cubby knew I was good at judging it and I took extra delight in gauging exactly the right spot while John and Ian were watching. The ferry squeezed the fender flat, pushing *Monaco* harmlessly and unscathed out of her path.

Cubby was unconcerned about the incident in the harbour and reassured the others. He liked her solidity. *Monaco* would do. She would be the one.

Later, in the hotel dining room, drawings were scattered amongst glasses and plates as John and Ian immersed themselves, meticulously planning the layout for cabins, bathrooms, drying room, galley and saloon for our prospective passengers. They revelled in details: little shelves for a book, a hook at face level to see your watch in the night, reading lights, lights inside hanging cupboards, two hooks for towels in the showers, a wine rack and book case in the saloon. Cubby said nothing, listening to the debate about what went where, how many inches each cabin could be. On and on they went, delving deeper and deeper into the minutiae of cabins, loos, showers and the drying room: everything had to fit in to what was now the fish hold. Eventually they were satisfied.

They had not only managed to fit everything in but had painstakingly drawn the cabins to scale on graph paper. John leant back complacently, picking up his glass he pushed the sketches across the table. 'Looks pretty good, don't you think, Cubby?' he said rather smugly. Cubby bent over the sheets. He burrowed in his pocket for his tin of tobacco, flipped it open, took out a green Rizla paper and slowly started to roll a cigarette. Silence. We all waited. Eventually, he looked up at John; I could tell a little smile was tugging at the corners of his mouth.

'Aye, aye, you've done a great job. Aye, it's a great job. It all looks just fine. But there's one wee thing. There's a cabin missing.'

Six

When we had first drawn into Peterhead after my father-in-law's funeral, John had told me it was possible *Monaco*'s insurers would reject our claim. They were doubtful: after all she'd only been on their books for one day before needing to be rescued. The tow, combined with the short-term repairs in Peterhead, had clocked up nearly twenty thousand pounds. 'Just find out what you can. We need to know why she was sinking, there's bound to be more to it,' he'd insisted. I'd never walked into a pub on my own, but I'd been told I would find our tug captain with a dram and a pint in the corner of the Creel Inn. He was swarthy and dark, and his huge powerful hands curled gently round the dram. Suspicion oozed out of him: what did this redhead want? But he was also a Yorkshireman, so much easier for me to understand than the thick Peterhead dialect I'd been struggling with.

After receiving John's instructions, he told me, he had left the safe harbour of Aberdeen in his tug to find the *Monaco*, a steam of over six hours through a black January night. *Monaco* when he reached her was rolling and wallowing from side to side, powerless in the big swells she had drifted amongst the brightly lit, humming rigs of the Ekofisk oil field. Circling round in the tug, he had made his assessment as he listened to the VHF transmissions coming from the *Monaco*'s crew.

'Mayday! Mayday! Mayday! **This is** *MONACO! MONACO! MONACO!*'

He watched her pitching aimlessly, water sloshing across her decks. As she rolled and wallowed, he had also been able to make out the blue light of a burning gas ring and to see figures huddled around, keeping warm. Snug in the crew's mess. So he had simply ignored the Mayday transmissions and instead instructed them to prepare *Monaco* for a tow and thus had saved us and our insurers from paying out salvage claims.

I could tell he was making light of a tough job with boats rolling heavily in the winter swells and I appreciated his Yorkshire sense of dogged perseverance. Something was needed. 'Could I have a dozen bottles of Grouse, please?' I asked the barman. 'Yes, in a box would be great!' He'd earned every one of them. Word went round the town. It was the first little crack in the carapace of local hostility.

Cubby had of course instructed me in great detail how to brief the delivery crew who were to bring *Monaco* to Scotland from her Danish home port. His long list of critical items had started with checking the bilge pumps and gone on to ensuring they had the appropriate charts. But with the difficulties of my father-in-law's death, the briefing had been cancelled. John and I had reasoned they must be OK – they were a professional delivery crew after all. But it seemed they had neither bothered to check the bilge pumps nor study the charts. In shallow Danish waters, *Monaco* had touched the bottom, knocking off a little pod housing the sensor for the echo sounder. Water flowed in through the small hole. A hole the size of a grapefruit and eventually, the engine room had become knee deep in greasy, cold saltwater. Death to an engine. However, the belts which drove her machinery, now wet, started to slip and the engine had come to a stop; no corrosive saltwater had been sucked in. *Monaco*, powerless, had drifted, with the wind pushing her within the 'cordon sanitaire' of a pulsating oil rig. Operations had been closed down, drilling stopped. It seemed the tug captain had not been our only piece of luck.

After *Monaco*'s arrival in Peterhead, we'd spent four long freezing weeks working on her. Exposed high above the concrete slipway, the biting easterly winter wind whistled round the hull, flurries of snow blew across her deck. Whether out in the howling winds, sloshing about in the bilges in freezing water or squeezed into the engine room, I had worked hard. Making her seaworthy again had occupied the engineers for three weeks while we'd worked on the non-technical things. We had temporarily repaired the damage caused by the towing cable, cleared debris from the decks, and scrubbed off ingrained oil, diesel and grime from the engine room, hydraulics and electrics. I thought I would never be warm or clean again. We'd lurked in cafes clasping hot mugs of coffee, steamed in the shower at the Fishermen's Mission and slept in pastel-hued

B&Bs while living on the best fish and chips in the world, and occasionally I had joined the shipwrights in their canteen, warming my bum by the gas heater, using the need to make calls on my wonderful mobile as an excuse.

While *Monaco* was exposed and totally visible on the slip out of the water, five marine surveyors came up to inspect and assess. Arrogant, chauvinistic or ingratiating, each had been convinced his plans were the best. Below the deck, in accordance with John's sketch in what was presently the vast fish hold, there were to be a small saloon, en suite cabins, and a drying room. Above deck we wanted a galley and dining saloon with big viewing windows. We needed a ship-yard that could do the work quickly and well and, as I'd been warned, would not go bust mid-conversion. We needed a surveyor I could trust and who would not take advantage of my inexperience. It was just the sort of project any one of them would relish. I hadn't a clue which one to choose, but eventually, using a combination of cost and gut feelings, I had made a decision. After discussions with John, we'd settled on one that was known for its proficiency with steel, vital for the proposed construction of the new deck saloon.

Between the surveyors' visits, two directors of our little company decided to come and see what was going on. In earlier days they had taken cruises with Kate and Cubby and so had invested on the strength of those holidays. One day, emerging from the fish hold, grimy and smelly, I found two men standing on deck amongst the twisted gear, staring around. One I recognised from our inspections in Denmark, the weedy streak, Ian, with a wobbling drip on the end of his nose. The other, a dapper little fellow, stretched out a hand. 'Hello! I'm Jeremy, ex-Navy don't ye know! Come to see what's what!'

For three days they got in the way. Jeremy fussed about getting dirty and Ian stood about useless and cold. Neither had any idea of what they could do to help and both were suspicious of me and impervious to my attempts to charm them.

'No!' said Jeremy at the suggestion he and Ian join us for supper. 'I will not join unwashed trawler men in the Fisherman's Mission to eat congealed pie and frozen peas! It's just not my kind of place!'

Cubby, concentrating on his roll-up, looked up. He began slowly, 'Do you know what the three most useless things on a boat are?' I held my breath knowing the answer well. 'Aye, well,' he went on, taking his time to insert the little filter into his roll-up. 'It'll be a top hat, a lawn mower and a naval officer.' Jeremy huffed his way down the ladder and was gone. John had one director the less.

'Aye, aye, away you go. I've told Cubby you can be off. She's ready now,' said Ali, the chief foreman at Stickers, as our engineers were known in Peterhead.

Shipwrights had caulked and pitched her hull and made her deck watertight again. Sparkies had reconditioned the electric motors needed for *Monaco*'s navigation lights and radar. Stickers' engineers had overhauled as much as was needed to get her going. Cubby had lashed the shattered fishing gear, tying it down so it was immoveable whatever winter swells we might encounter. And now Ali said *Monaco* was ready to go. It seemed terrifying.

Ali was reassuringly calm; I trusted him completely. Small and neat, he was the perfect size for a ship's engineer. His face and hands had a deep oily diesel sheen making him look like a dedicated sunbather, but occasionally when he pushed aside his cap a luminous white bald dome glowed underneath: engine rooms are sunless places. A devout Baptist, he was as clean living at home as he was grimy during the day, and, as chief foreman with a workforce of two hundred, he was a firm but fair God. If he said the *Monaco* was safe, she was; and while the idea of actually being in the North Sea in January was terrifying, I was desperate to get on to the next stage of the venture. We had just three months to transform her into a smart expedition ship carrying twelve lucky passengers. The solid industrial ugly duckling designed for Arctic waters had to turn into a sleek swan. We had the prestigious National Trust for Scotland contract to honour, plus *Monaco* was to offer expedition cruises on Scotland's treach-erous west coast.

I sauntered out of the workshop, trying to appear happy with the news and there she was, calmly tied up alongside the quay. 'OK. Let's get going.' My voice sounded wobbly even to me. 'Ali's told me we can go. He's already told Cubby and the harbour master,' I said to Kate. 'So let's get going.'

There was not a sign of Cubby.

'Do you know where he is, Kate? He said last night the tide'd be OK so we'd better get on with it.' She said nothing but disappeared into the crew mess aft. I peered up into the wheelhouse. No sign of him.

Then he came round the corner of the ice plant, walking slowly under the massive stainless-steel chute which disgorged the ice, to shoot it straight into the hold of a waiting trawler; it was the last thing each ship did before heading off to catch more fish. Cubby paused and stared at the *Monaco*, no roll-up to be seen. Without a word, he jumped lightly onto the deck and disappeared into the engine room.

A giant cough shook *Monaco*. *Boom! Boom! Boom!* A great spurt of cooling water spouted into the harbour from the pipe in her port side: *Monaco* came to life.

She was still a mess, with her deck more of an assault course than a clear, neat working space. Jagged pieces of superstructure and twisted fishing gear were a sharp reminder of the damage she'd suffered from the tow across the North Sea. As the deck throbbed gently, I considered Ali's comment that she had the Rolls Royce of marine engines. All five cylinders beat purposefully. He should know, so who was I to doubt?

Kate and I stood on deck, now unable to hide our grins, one on the starboard and one on the port shoulder, each of us with a fender in hand.

Ali, his apprentices and the shipwrights were lined up to look down at us from the quay. Figures in yellow oilskins stood up and stared across the harbour. Bustling forklift trucks paused as the drivers peered out of their cabs at us. There were people lining the harbour, standing, staring, waiting. The whole town knew about the red-haired English girl; there'd even been a piece in the *Press and Journal* about me.

The *Monaco* began to move.

Slowly she rubbed her starboard side along the quay.

Sideways, like a crab, she scraped along, blown by the chill January wind.

Minutes passed.

Steadily she moved on along the quay edge, drifting remorselessly on. I glanced up, as the shadow of the massive hollow ice chute came closer and closer. Any moment now *Monaco*'s mast would bash right into it, dragging it off at the roots.

On she drifted.

The throb through my feet become a smooth regular beat and at last, steadily, purposefully, *Monaco* began to inch astern, backing away from the chute. A gap opened up between her starboard gunwale and the edge of the quay. Slowly her stem turned away from the stone coping towards the opening in the dock wall. She inched her way gently through the narrow cutting under the first swing bridge and into the second basin, steadily past swing bridge number two, moving through the maze of basins and swing bridges that were safe home to the great fishing fleet of Peterhead.

The people lining the quays stared, but no one waved or smiled. Silently they watched. Waiting for *Monaco* to collide with a fishing boat, to run into the harbour wall or for Cubby to take a wrong turn and miss the exit. But unhurriedly he gently eased her delicately through the armada of fishing boats and past the harbour master's office windows. Cheekily, I waved. That would teach them to think we were amateurs.

We were clear. Out into the North Sea and neither of us had needed to use a fender. I looked up at the wheelhouse windows and blew Cubby a kiss.

Once the course had been set, the engine room checked and we were all standing for the first time on our moving boat, I asked him, 'OK then, where were you?'

'Aye, well.' He looked at me, grinning. 'I needed to find a toilet — she's a big boaty.' I knew he'd skippered smart luxury yachts as well as fishing boats and had worked at sea all his life, but I hadn't realised until then that *Monaco* was the biggest boat he had ever handled. Weaving through the convoluted harbour and its interlocking basins, narrow channels and swing bridges, was challenging even when you knew your boat well, and he'd had no idea how *Monaco* would turn and 'drive': in some places there had only been inches to spare.

'I thought the mast was going to knock the ice chute off! Were you asleep?' I went on, teasing him.

'No, I'd forgotten to put her into gear,' he admitted with a broad grin.

Grey Peterhead with its tightly packed streets began to slip astern as *Monaco* headed north, nosing into a lazy rolling swell: not bad for the North Sea in the depths of winter. Our final destination was round on the west coast, south of the Clyde, the little fishing port of Troon, where the shipyard chosen to transform *Monaco* was based. To get there would take four days, and first we had to round exposed Rattray Head, then steam almost due west to pass Buckie and Macduff, on into the Cromarty Firth eight hours away, where the entrance to the Caledonian Canal waited. Slicing through the Highlands, the canal would save us at least two days, with its inland lochs of Ness and Oich and flight of eight locks known as Neptune's Staircase tucked under the watchful gaze of Ben Nevis, before we reached the open sea again by Fort William. Once out of the canal, we would go due south down Loch Linnhe, have the shelter of the islands of Mull, Kerrera, Scarba and Jura, before we took on the exposed complicated tides round the Mull of Kintyre, finally crossing the entrance to the Clyde, to arrive in Troon. Even in summer it was a demanding route and now in the depths of winter we needed good weather, but it was also potentially a beautiful as well as an exciting voyage.

Monaco steamed on; we had rounded Rattray Head and, as the dark drew in, Cubby turned the wheel to head her west. There was no one about, no specks of nearby boats showing green on the radar, just an occasional distant light from the fishing communities and little harbours of Buckie and Macduff away to port, all too shallow to offer shelter to *Monaco*. Cubby, closing one eye to keep his night vision, lit another cigarette. Kate and I were squeezed onto the narrow seat next to the useless echo sounder. The atmosphere was crisp with tension. We knew nothing of this boat. We couldn't even read the instrument labels; everything was in Danish. From the battered fishing gear, tightly lashed to the deck, to the engine pulsing away beneath our feet, we had no experience of any of *Monaco*'s machinery. We were dirty, weary, hungry and cold, but sitting in the red-and-green glow from the navigation lights there was no question of a watch rota, it was far too exciting. *Monaco* steadily and surely was making her way towards Troon and we grinned at each other in the shadowy instrument glow.

Suddenly, the steady rhythmic beat of the engine was shattered by an ear-piercing wail. A bright red light flashed urgently on a small black box close to the instrument panel. ON! OFF! ON! OFF! A siren screamed out from above our heads.

'What the fuck?' shouted Cubby above the din. Grabbing the torch he'd carefully placed within reach, he shone it at the box and flipped up the main control switch next to the red light.

Silence.

It was possible to think now, but the red light flashed insistently. He shone the torch on the dials. Oil pressure, engine revs, and propeller pitch – the needles were all steady. Nothing had changed. I too peered at the black box. Each light had a neat clear label, in Danish. 'Keep her head into the swell, Katie, and I'll go and have a look.' Kate took over, glancing at the radar to see if anything was near.

'All the paperwork I found I've pushed into those little drawers, I'll see if I can find anything,' I volunteered, anxious to be doing something. Cubby had disappeared to the engine room and Kate stood at the wheel, turning it occasionally to keep *Monaco*'s head into the swell as she kept a wary eye on the radar. The red light went on flashing. On–off. On–off.

Dragging my own torch from my jeans pocket, I stuck it in my mouth to free my hands and tugged at the damp little drawers in the skipper's cabin immediately behind the wheelhouse. There had been no time to decipher any of the muddled mass of papers and John had promised to send a Danish dictionary to Troon. The masses of yellowing sheets were indecipherable; Danish had not seemed a language I would need at school. There were faded diagrams too including one sheet headed '*Electriks*'. I studied the wiring diagram's spidery lines. Number five was the flashing one: '*Tåghorn*'. Horn must be horn in any language.

'Kate, I think it might be the horn,' I said doubtfully.

'Aye, well, maybe just find the fucking fuse for number five,' was her terse reply. I knelt on plastic floor matting, torch in mouth and fumbled at the back of the box amongst the bundles of wires. Cubby appeared from the engine room.

'There's no problem down there. It's all OK.'

'I think it's the horn, Cubby.'

'OK, pull the damn thing out and we'll soon know,' was the response. Hoping I'd got the right one, I twiddled the knurled nut and pulled out the fuse. Cubby returned the switch to its rightful place. No lights came on, nothing flashed. All was silent. No blaring siren. All that fright for a short circuit in the horn.

Early next morning, with no further incidents, we made it to the canal. In the watery early morning light Cubby carefully nudged *Monaco* into the sea lock; she might be a mess, with chewed-up steel and smashed fishing gear, but she was his command and he was already proud of her. Safe in the canal, we were greeted as *Monaco* progressed through locks by Kate and Cubby's friends; they had friends everywhere. One of the loch keepers shouted out.

'Och, it's yourselves! And how're you doing in yon big boaty?' Our curious pale blue, battered fishing boat, so unlike the regular Scottish ones they knew so well, was already starting to make her mark.

Going through the locks was of course another art I had to learn as the wind pushed on *Monaco*'s superstructure, pinning her against the wall while the water flowed in, lifting her up. At the last gate before Loch Ness, the keeper's wife stretched across the gap passing fluffy white baps stuffed with bacon into our hands. *Monaco* chugged steadily across the dark waters of Loch Ness, making light of the strong south-westerly winter wind and heavy rain.

A very slight change of note unsettled us all. The engine missed a beat. Another. A little cough. Then silence.

Silently *Monaco* drifted over the ink-black surface of Loch Ness. Gusts of wind and blasts of wintry rain swooped down from the surrounding hills, pummelling her.

'You, get out on deck and keep a look out,' I was told. 'Kate, keep her head into the wind.' Not so easy, as the surrounding Highlands increased the strength of the irregular gusts pushing the *Monaco* remorselessly towards the shore. It was getting dark, we had no lifejackets or life rafts and even though it was a loch, it was deep. Monaco would be wrecked.

On deck the wind and rain were fierce, but I thought I could just hear the faint chug of an engine as I peered through the rain squall. A red navigation light glowed. Cubby appeared from the engine room, as ever in heavy yellow oilskins. He swiftly jumped up onto the bulwark and then to the top of the huge red whaleback. Like a sort of steel umbrella, it usually sheltered the men while they sorted the catch on deck, but now it gave him height. It was slippery in the rain and there were evil spikes of aluminium sticking up where the tow cable had ripped it. I wanted to shout to him to be careful, he might slip, fall off, or cut his leg. But of course he'd spent most of his life on slippery decks.

Cubby had absolutely refused to go to sea without one good rope. He and I had spent hours searching through scrap yards in Peterhead and Aberdeen, as the type he wanted was extremely expensive. He had firm ideas on what he wanted, its length and composition, and eventually we'd found one, lying rejected behind a shed, coiled up like a lifeless anaconda. He'd swapped it for some of the *Monaco*'s fishing gear and had stowed it under the whaleback: ready, in case.

By now, the gap between *Monaco* and the approaching boat was about thirty feet; the rope was plaited, multi-stranded and as thick as my arm. I'd seen him throw a rope before and always admired the skill, but now it was vital: *Monaco* was nearing the shore. He made a few small swings judging the weight of it, then the rope was snaking out, uncurling across the gap. A figure standing on the other boat's whaleback caught it and made fast. Cubby knew it had to be our rope, otherwise the *Silver Darling* could have claimed salvage, a practice rarely pursued amongst fishing boats but *Monaco* was an oddity, so you never knew.

Tightly lashed together, *Monaco* was towed for the second time in her short life with us. Embarrassingly, she had simply run out of diesel. Her fuel system turned out to have yet another cunning piece of Danish design. There was no need for costly manholes in the fuel tanks: if the fuel flowed continuously through them, you didn't need to open them up and check for sludge. Sludge had no chance to collect, but she did need to have enough fuel. We had everything to learn about her.

From the calm of the Lock Inn at Fort Augustus, I rang John to report in. He was not amused. 'How could you have run out of fuel? Why on earth didn't you fill her up?'

Smugly, I quoted Cubby. 'Well, full tanks are really heavy and that would be a big weight on the hull when she goes into dry dock in Troon, and that's not good for her frame. Cubby's trying to be careful with costs too, you know.'

John recognised when he'd lost. 'Well, we've a board meeting on Thursday at the Grahams' in Wiltshire and you need to be here: everyone wants to know what's going on. Ian's complaining, and of course Jeremy's already had his money back. We've got to calm the others down, so no more dramas. Today's Tuesday; if you leave tomorrow you can get here in the evening ready for the meeting the next morning.'

Loch Ness to Wiltshire in a day! He had no idea. Public transport was a joke at the height of summer, never mind in the depths of winter. Rather to my annoyance, Cubby seemed unperturbed. 'Aye, aye, well, then, we'll just have to stop the Mallaig train.'

At three o'clock next morning in the pitch dark he stood in the middle of the track. I could hear the train approaching: quickly it rounded the corner. Cubby just stood there, in his yellow oilskins, calmly swinging the none-too bright torch back and forth. The train slowed and then stopped. No drama, no screeching brakes, quietly it just rolled to a stop. A head stuck out of the driver's window. 'Och. It's yourself! How's your boaty? I hear she's not so good. Do you think you'll be keeping her?'

Reaching up, I opened a door and clambered in whilst Cubby chatted to the engine driver about the strength and charms of the *Monaco*. I was completely exhausted, worn out by cold and frights, by negotiating with surveyors and shipyards and dealing with engineers and sparkies for our already beloved *Monaco*.

After three changes of train and a taxi to the village, I arrived at the carved sixteenth-century oak door of the Grahams' house. I could hear a phone ringing as Fanny opened the door. Behind her, James answered it.

'Yes. Hello, this is James. Oh, Cubby! Good. Good. We've been waiting to hear from you. Oh, you're short of money. No more change. OK, I can call you back. What's the number? No? Are you sure? All right then. Yes, she's just arrived. I will pass on the message. Good night then.'

'Hello, Fanny. It's lovely to be here. Hello, James. How are you? Did Cubby have anything important to say?' I asked nervously. John appeared and gave me a hug. Other people, who I assumed were shareholders or directors, stood about in the hall looking expectant.

Finally James said casually, 'Yes, that was Cubby. They've arrived in Troon and *Monaco*'s safely tied up. She goes up the slip in the morning ready to start the work.'

That was it. No dramas. I almost felt angry. None of them would understand how frightening it had all been: being blown towards the shore; the cold, the dark and the exhaustion. But what did it matter? *Monaco*'s transformation was about to begin.

Seven

I moved like a chameleon: a hand, then a foot, gingerly edging my way along the level horizontal ladder. Below me yawned a thirty-foot hole, lined with unforgiving concrete: the bottom of the dry dock. A heavy plastic supermarket bag swung from under my wrist, making me increasingly unstable. I'd nearly made it, just a few more rungs to negotiate, when there was a shout from below and I froze, looking down. 'You'll no be getting far with only a wee poly bag for your weekend.' I opened my mouth to retort that it held six thousand pounds which would keep me going quite happily for a couple of days but thought better of it. 'Yes, you're probably right, but I think I'll be here for the weekend anyway, not much chance of the bright lights yet! See you later.' I could sense the shipwright working under *Monaco*'s hull, watching my bum as I jumped down from the ladder before making my way through the deserted streets to the Clydesdale Bank.

At last the conversion was progressing well and although it was just two months since she'd arrived there, things finally seemed to be going smoothly.

John and the directors were enjoying my reports, progress was steady and the goal of 6th May for the first National Trust charter seemed possible. As I sauntered into Troon's only bank, I realised this was fun: I was busy, and there was no time to dwell on Digby's death. I knew Hugo was happy. After submitting his portfolio, he'd succeeded in bagging a prestigious art scholarship.

Inside the solid Victorian red-brick building, a lone cashier was tucked behind the counter. I dumped the bag in front of her and began to count out the six thousand pounds, in dirty individual pound notes, one by one. She didn't bat an eyelid. No questions, no sign of surprise. Big wodges of cash were clearly the norm in fishing communities.

Monaco would not need the cumbersome fishing gear in her new role and Cubby had insisted that we sell it all. It was worth good money, he said, which should be in our pockets, not the shipyard's. The advert in the *Fishing News* had precisely described all the various pieces *Monaco* had once used. First was the huge main winch which stretched across the whole deck; you could just squeeze between each end and the gunwale. Fifteen-foot wide, and in five sections, its drums turned independently to wind up the steel hawsers attached to the bag net of the trawl, a massive dead weight when full of fish. At the stern, bolted to the gunwales, were the gallows, one on each side – seven-foot high and shaped like a giant letter 'A'. As the bag net was winched in, the hawsers attached to the trawl were pulled up over the gallows which guided them onto the drums of the winch. The solid weight of the catch was thus kept evenly distributed across the *Monaco* to ensure she remained stable in big seas. Finally, there was the mangled whaleback, the giant aluminium umbrella that gave the crew a degree of shelter from the icy spray as they stood sorting the catch on the heaving deck. The fish had to be divided into different types, depending on size and value; they were then posted into *Monaco*'s hold through holes cut in the deck. Each opening was about eighteen inches in diameter and had a removable metal plate that could be locked shut to keep out the sea. Underneath each hole, the fish hold was divided into sections by boards, known as pound boards: each board slotted into metal frames to create compartments to hold the slippery fish. Without dividing up the catch, the whole slithering mass would have been able to slip from side to side, again making *Monaco* unstable.

Specifically designed for trawling the cold rich waters of the far north, she would have left Søndeborg full of ice to come home crammed with fish with the deck at her 'waist' actually underwater. Sometimes it took just a few days to fill her cavernous, forty-five-foot hold, sometimes over two weeks. She was an efficient, solid oak fishing machine, designed from years of experience to deal with mountainous Arctic seas and massive weights of fish. Her conversion into a charming little passenger ship was progressing as completely as my own conversion and I could feel my country-house life slipping away as I turned into shipyard foreman and decision maker. From bilge pump impellors to radar scanners, echo sounders, life rafts and anodes: I was learning they were all vital but I still needed to know why.

'Hello. Yes, of course you're welcome to come and make an inspection,' I had replied to our potential fishing gear purchaser. 'Yes, in Troon in the dry dock.' While *Monaco* had travelled from Peterhead, through the Caledonian Canal, word had spread all around the west coast, so undoubtedly whoever he was would be inquisitive. *Monaco* looked exposed and sort of naked, propped up in the dry dock with no sea to clothe her, and no doubt the Oban fishing mafia would like to know more. However, when Angus MacDonald arrived it turned out he and Cubby had known each other for years, had blethered about the weather and tatties over the VHF and not just sunk drams in the Oban Arms. He liked the winch and gallows and, after some formulaic haggling over the price, Cubby made had him take the whaleback too. Curiously he had brought exactly the right money with him, six thousand pounds in fish-whiffy, crumpled one pound notes. Cubby had insisted Kate and I should count the 'spondulix' while he and Angus caught up with a dram or two.

Although *Monaco* was making progress, time was short and I had learnt that shipyards seemed to be governed by breaks – coffee, lunch, tea. Every couple of hours, it seemed, the workforce stopped: I longed for them just to get on with it. Yet *Monaco* was steadily changing. The unglamorous industrial trawler was being transformed into a sturdy expedition ship through what Cubby referred to as 'London ways': John's financial nous and air of calm stability, plus a smart suit, had achieved a marine mortgage from the Clydesdale Bank, as well as grants and loans from the Highlands & Islands Development Board. All wanted regular reports, so progress needed to be tangible, and I was learning to weave a path between the lackadaisical shipyard and the bureaucratic Department of Transport who would eventually issue the licence to allow *Monaco* to work.

Four months earlier, before we bought *Monaco*, I had made the first of many visits to the greatly feared Department of Transport. Without the licences, one for the boat and one for the skipper, *Monaco* could not move – but for a boat of her size the rules were fluid, nothing was written, everything was 'a grey area'. I gathered that each surveyor could interpret the rules as he chose, reflecting his own particular obsessions and fetishes. Some had views on thickness of window glass, others on how the hatches should close. Exemptions were permitted, but they were at the whim of the appointed inspector and *Monaco* would be required to meet these safety regulations. Not that these were trivial. The west coast with its liberal scattering of submerged rocks and skerries was well known to be extremely hazardous and we would be carrying people.

In addition to the boat, each skipper had to have his own licence issued by the Department of Trade recognising his abilities, local knowledge and experience. Fortunately, Cubby had been skippering similar boats all over the west coast for more than sixteen years, so he already had a licence from the Department and we didn't expect any worries there. But it was vital to know if the Department would approve *Monaco* and that she would be given her certificate to operate with passengers.

Adrian, our swivel-eyed marine surveyor, who had done the survey in Denmark, had advised against visiting the Department. 'Get going. You need to get on if there's a chance of meeting the National Trust deadline. You can deal with the vagaries of the Department later. That's what everyone does. That's the way it's done,' he urged. But as a judge's daughter I had no fear of the bureaucrats in Glasgow and I was determined not to be caught out. Cubby had regaled me with tales of boats which, after extensive refits, had failed to be given a licence. This was not going to happen to us.

So, before we bought *Monaco* and went to the expense of going to Denmark, I had visited the Department, taking her particulars and the proposed deck plans. The bare cream-painted office had reminded me of school, with the same sensation of waiting for the headmistress. I sat by the large mahogany desk as weak sunlight shone through the metal-framed window onto a wall poster covered with curious symbols. The anchors and buoys were easy to understand, but much of the rest were simply a collection of unknown squiggles and marks. I gazed around, looking at the desk, but there were no papers, just a brass metal tray holding four clear plastic Bic biros lying side-by-side, cosily snuggled up, tips exactly aligned. There was a green one, a red one, a blue and a black. Each had a small piece of paper with something scribbled in the appropriate colour tucked inside the clear barrel with the bung carefully pushed back into place. I picked up the red one and peered at the writing. Inscribed in red ink was the single word *Potts*. Suddenly the door opened and I jumped, caught, biro in hand. A tall, thin-lipped man, pale with the translucence of an indoor life, entered. He had a trim little clipped beard and close-set eyes. I carefully put the biro back in the tray and stood up, stretching out my hand. 'Good morning,' I ventured.

'And good morning, to you, too. I'm Captain Potts.'

His prim Morningside Edinburgh accent matched the biros. My heart sank. He looked just as neat and precise and I wondered if it would be possible to get this formal Scot on my side. Flirting clearly wasn't an option; I would just have to be neat and precise too.

'Captain Potts, thank you for seeing me. I've come to ask the Department's advice about a boat the company I represent is thinking of purchasing.' I didn't want him to think it was just me, not just an English girl with a whim. 'We are hoping the boat will be suitable for a licence to operate on the west coast,' I declared firmly. He didn't look like a social chit-chat sort of fellow.

'Well, let me see.'

Carefully – I didn't want to flick the biros for six – I unfolded the A3 diagrams of the *Monaco* and spread them over his desk. He peered through his gold-rimmed glasses, studying the drawings. I waited, silently. No feminine gabbling. This was professional stuff and maybe he'd interpret my silence as deference.

Eventually, he leaned back folding the glasses slowly, before laying them down at the side of his desk. 'Aye, she looks fine. She has an acceptable hull and I see she's Danish? I don't think we have any Danish vessels operating on the west coast. She could make it up to

89

a Class VIIIA. Yes, that would be good. Class VIIIA is what all these small passenger boats should be. I don't hold with Exemptions.'

I vaguely remembered a Class VIIIA was what Cubby had mentioned, but no exemptions sounded demanding. I pressed on: 'We're proposing to employ Mr MacKinnon as the skipper. I think you know him, Captain Potts, he's been skippering on the west coast for some years now and has a licence from the Department. He was born on Jura,' I added, anxious to emphasise Cubby's local knowledge. 'Will he be OK to be in charge?'

'Yes, the Department's known Mr MacKinnon for quite a while now, so there'll be no problems there. We know he's been out at St Kilda many a time with the National Trust parties,' he said.

As the work on *Monaco* had progressed, I and even Cubby, who loathed anything that represented authority, grudgingly came to respect the pedantic and precise Captain Potts. He was continuously and never-endingly cautious and meticulous. But if he was a constant thorn in our sides, he was a complete thorn bush to the shipyard. He ensured nothing was omitted, no corners were cut and he checked every little thing over and over again, ensuring everything was up to speed. Surprisingly he and Cubby seemed to get on well, sitting in the crew mess drinking endless mugs of coffee, discussing ship construction and marine engines. Cubby was good company and when he chose was adept at turning up the charm especially when he knew it was necessary. Potts recognised Cubby's practical skills and admired his seamanship, not to mention his knowledge of futtock knees and freeing ports. Cubby despised Potts's lack of experience at the sharp end. He was a desk captain in Cubby's eyes, but Potts never had an inkling that Cubby was simply sucking up to him.

Having lodged the six thousand grubby one pound notes at the bank, I strolled back through the colourless Victorian streets to the shipyard. I felt cheerful. Things were going well on the *Monaco:* she was rapidly changing from an ugly duckling. I reckoned we'd make it on time for the National Trust even if all the workers had knocked off for the weekend. We had plenty to do and I would be able to send a good report: John would be pleased.

As I neared the dry dock, a sound of screeching, wrenching timber shattered the peace. As fast as I dared, I launched myself back along the horizontal ladder. The quicker I went the more it bounced over the concrete hole. I began to feel really grumpy. I had been fantasising about soaking in a bath and maybe supper in the neon-lit Chinese restaurant, Troon's finest.

'Hi, Kate, what the hell's happening? What's that horrific noise?'

Kate looked defensive, wary. 'Aye, well, you're not to take it bad. He's away below. Down in the hold with the fire axe.'

The sides of the hull in the fish hold were lined with pine planking and Adrian's plans showed this wooden panelling as being cleaned and polished to make stylish walls for the passenger cabins. But Cubby had insisted we needed to know what was behind the panelling. He argued there might be hidden rot or burrowing worms weakening *Monaco*'s hull. We had to know before we built the cabins, fixed the walls and installed the heating, plumbed in wash basins and loos. Loud, heated arguments between Cubby and Adrian had concluded with Adrian insisting he knew best. He was a surveyor. He knew and was adamant that once disturbed the panelling would not fit back into place, and of course it would look fantastically smart when polished up. Besides, it would save considerable expense. Cubby had been threatening to get behind the planks for some days and he'd obviously taken the opportunity while I was out of the way at the bank.

Kate watched as I disappeared through the hatch down yet another ladder into the dark of the fish hold. My stomach heaved. The stink was sickening. It was so strong I gasped. Rank, cloying, a stench of decaying fish, rancid tallow and diesel fumes burnt my nostrils. A naked bulb, hanging from a nail under the deck, illuminated a medieval tableau on the far side. All around was inky black. Cubby, in grimy yellow oilskins, feet braced against the curve of the hull, swung the axe again and again, slicing deep into the pine.

He was clearly in a rage and was quite likely to hurl down the axe in a fury and tell me that our surveyor was a 'pillock', that the whole project was ridiculous and that I knew nothing about boats. It had happened before. I waited. I needed to be careful.

'Aye, aye, it's yourself!' he growled. I've always liked this Scottish greeting, sort of non-committal, stating the obvious but not actually even saying hello, just acknowledging a presence.

'Yes. I've put the money in the bank, no problem. They didn't even ask, not a word, not one single question about where it came from.' I could hardly breathe with the stink and he must be finding it bad too. 'How about a cuppa?' I ventured.

He didn't move and clearly was not going to be fobbed off with that. I stepped warily towards him over the pools of water that lay in the uneven fish-hold floor. 'Can you see the hull now? And the frames too?' I asked. No point in pretending I didn't know what he was doing.

'No. I cannae see a goddamn fucking thing. Just black slime and I can't breathe either. Let's get out of here. Out of this fuckin' stench.'

We clambered up, gasping for fresh air as the kettle whistled. Canny Kate must have been listening. Fortified by coffee, I put on my oilskins and Cubby grabbed the big yellow torch: I followed him back down the ladder.

The reek was indescribable.

Cubby swung the axe again and again. I watched horrified as the wooden planking screeched and split apart. But he was very careful and his aim was perfect. Only the panelling between the frames splintered. Soon a large area was split open. With gloved hands he pulled away the splinters of wood and I shone the torch into the jagged black hole. Every surface glistened. Evil black slime shone wickedly all over the hull and the frames, every part was covered in it.

'Let's get out of here. I can't breathe or even think

with this stench,' I said, turning round, desperate to get out into the fresh air.

We did have supper in the Chinese, but despite a shower in our B&B there was a lingering pong; it seemed impossible to get it out of our noses. I wasn't hungry. How I was going to explain this to John away in London? He would not appreciate Cubby attacking *Monaco*'s hull with an axe, or that I had let him ignore Adrian's expensive advice.

Monaco was supposed to be ready in eight weeks for her first passengers. I imagined the chaos if we had followed Adrian's advice, completed the transformation and sailed away, possibly with the heating on full blast to air the boat. Only then would that smell have come wafting out of the cabin walls, seeping through the pretty panelling. We had to find out what was causing it.

In the morning, I plucked up courage and called John. Sensibly, he recognised he was too far removed from the action. His response was one I was increasingly familiar with: 'Get it sorted out, deal with it.' I could tell he was running out of patience. Cubby, he said, 'had taken unilateral action'. Any more problems and John would call a halt.

Our poor *Monaco* appeared to be in a concrete coffin. No one would work on her. The dry dock surrounding her supporting cradle was silent. The lads had simply refused to go into the hold, walking away saying it was impossible to breathe or work in the stench.

We embarked on the job and four solid, stinking unremitting days later we had scraped every inch of the hold. Cubby removed all the panelling and the three of us had worked around the frames and right up under the deck. We steadily scraped away, cleaning off every bit of goo by hand. We could only stand the stench for an hour at a time before being overwhelmed by nausea, but we worked at it, night and day. After all, it was pitch black down there whatever the time was. Eventually, after we'd burnt our clothes – oilskins, boots, gloves and all – we went for a walk along the beach. It was, it seemed, yet another fiendish Danish trick. No air could get at the surfaces if they were plastered in goo. No air therefore no rot; no wonder Cubby's knife had not sunk into her hull.

Throughout the conversion, Potts had come and gone every few days, sticking his nose in everywhere, though curiously he hadn't been perturbed about the stench and we made sure he never knew about the asbestos insulation. If he'd found that, *Monaco* would have been condemned. We'd clawed out every little bit of that too. It was a constant battle, each surprise seeming worse than the last one but eventually, *Monaco* was complete. She had seven cabins with reading lights and little bookshelves, fluffy duvets, peach-coloured towels, flannels and shower curtains. There was a drying room and a neat saloon with smart tartan cushions. On deck, in front of the wheelhouse, was a custom-built brand new steel deckhouse containing a carefully fitted stainless-steel galley and dining saloon with raised seats to give passengers clear views through the huge windows. Sea trials had been done with Potts in attendance in the waters off Ailsa Craig. We had tested fire alarms, gas alarms, bilges alarms and engine room alarms. Run out the fire hoses, tested the bilge pumps and watertight doors, hoisted the daylight signals for 'at anchor' and 'not under command', practised the man-overboard drill, swung the compass and done the stability tests. Potts watched everything. The *Monaco* had passed and Potts had granted her the coveted licence. She had achieved the revered Class VIIIA, and with no Exemptions. At last she was ready: we could go. In spite of everything we were only one week late. We could make the National Trust deadline if we left Troon immediately.

We were almost too tired to be excited. It was a transformation but still only a beginning.

With the shipwrights gone, the decks now clear, *Monaco* lay quietly in the harbour waiting as Cubby, cautious as ever, checked there were no stray rags in the engine room that might block a bilge pump, or tools left lying around to cause a problem. All was ready, ropes neatly coiled, fenders carefully stowed. A smell of fresh paint lingered: Kate and I had just completed painting MONACO round the lifebelts. We had a ten-hour passage ahead of us, north across the mouth of the Clyde, around the Mull of Kintyre, up past Jura and Crinan and finally to Oban.

My eye was caught by a tall man walking quickly towards us down the quay: the unmistakable figure of Potts. My heart jumped. But there was nothing to be frightened of. The *Monaco* was a fully certificated passenger-carrying boat now and it was nice of him to come and see us off. I shouted up cheerfully, 'Hello, Captain Potts. Nice to see you! We're just setting off for Oban, Cubby wants to catch the tide around the Mull and with any luck we should be in Oban with a day to spare before the first National Trust people arrive for St Kilda.'

He stopped on the edge of the quay, looking down at me and then surprisingly started to make his way down the ladder until he stood on the deck between me and the wheelhouse.

'You will not be leaving with Mr MacKinnon in charge. Mr MacKinnon does not have the full qualifications. There'll be no going to sea until you have someone on board who does have the full qualifications.'

Eight

I stared at Potts. Before we bought *Monaco* he had agreed that Cubby would be our skipper. All I had to do was remind him about that meeting and his agreement and it would not be a problem, but if Cubby overheard I knew there'd be trouble. He was in the engine room making last-minute checks.

'Captain Potts, please can we discuss this off the boat. I'll join you in the café by the entrance to the shipyard, if you don't mind.' Not a fool, he returned to the quay but stood waiting for me to join him.

I stuck my head into the engine room door, 'I've just got a couple of bits of paperwork to sort out with Captain Potts, Cubby. I'll be back in a moment. Won't be long,' I shouted through the gap in the metal plating of the engine room. I could see his head below me as he checked the bilges and prayed that he had not heard anything; I knew he would have heard the footsteps on deck. His voice came from the depths: 'Aye, aye, it's OK. I've a wee bit to see to here before we go, but don't be long.'

I almost pushed Potts along the quay chattering

about the harbour, fishing boats, prawn creels, ropes, the weather, anything so he wouldn't have a chance to speak, and to get him out of Kate's earshot too.

Potts, who didn't have to explain himself, would say little, merely insisting that Cubby didn't have the correct qualifications and that with him in charge *Monaco* was not going anywhere. Even without fare-paying passengers, she still couldn't move if Cubby was in charge. I realised getting angry would achieve nothing.

'But Captain Potts, do you not remember our meeting last autumn? Before we bought her I asked your opinion on both the *Monaco* and Cubby. You told me the Department had known him for a long time and were happy with his experience. I even confirmed it to you by letter afterwards.' He looked down at his neat, highly polished black shoes and then gazed out of the window at the harbour. He looked anywhere, everywhere, except at me. And he looked evasive, not something I had ever seen in him before. Something was going on; he looked distinctly uncomfortable.

'Captain Potts,' I persisted, 'please explain to me what is wrong with Mr MacKinnon as skipper? You agreed he would be OK. You know we've the National Trust people coming in three days' time and I've promised them that *Monaco* will be ready. You've given her the certificate and their people are coming on board in Oban to go to St Kilda. We've done all you asked, please be kind enough to explain?'

He was immoveable. Cubby wouldn't do. The *Monaco* was fine. Cubby was the problem, I had to find someone else, someone with full qualifications, a master mariner, then she could move.

How would I tell Cubby that he was not allowed to skipper the boat he'd been promised? Not allowed to work. Not allowed to do what he'd been doing for years. Not allowed to be in charge of the boat he'd worked on so hard for the last four months. Anyone would be furious, but I knew him well enough to know his Celtic sense of doom would take over; it would be a portent for the whole venture. He might well throw in the towel and just wander off.

But there was no way of wrapping it up. I tried to make it sound like just a brief setback, a bureaucratic error that I could fix quickly. Predictably he went to the pub and Kate went with him. I rang John. John said he would see what he could do to find a master mariner.

Two days later, Kate and I were sitting in the wheelhouse waiting and watching. Cubby was sleeping, he'd simply opted out, and the *Monaco* was still in Troon, tied up at the main quay in the harbour. John, who'd handled the National Trust brilliantly, had persuaded them to give us time; they had postponed the first trip for three days.

'There they are.' I jumped down. 'Come on, let's go and meet them.'

'You go. I'll catch you later.' It was all a mess and Kate was fed up too.

Much to everyone's surprise, Ian, our limp director, had come up trumps. Amongst the regulars at his local pub was a master mariner, a fellow propper-up of the bar who would be happy to stand in. Here they were, arriving in Ian's white Mercedes. I wondered what he would be like. How would he get on with Cubby? Would Cubby even appear?

I walked along the quay towards the Merc as Ian uncoiled himself from the driver's seat. The passenger door opened and out popped our knight in shining armour: small, dark and hairy, with an unattractive-looking dark patch at the crotch of his trousers.

'Hello, Ian. Good drive?' I ventured.

'Get this Welshman to a toilet, fast!'

Not even a 'hello,' or an introduction. It seemed our knight was incontinent: he had peed on the white leather passenger seat of Ian's pride and joy. The final part of the drive from Birmingham had been spent with him sitting on a newspaper: that was soggy too. I tried not to grin. This would cheer Cubby up no end. The Welsh knight smiled and held out his hand; he didn't look like being much of a threat. We walked slowly down the quay to *Monaco* – after all, there were smart new electric loos on board. Our little Welsh saviour seemed totally unconcerned either by Ian's ill humour or his wet trousers. Kate, managing to keep the grin off her face, took him below to one of the smart new cabins to change. Cubby, having heard footsteps on deck, was sitting in the little mess, mug of coffee in hand, roll-up in the other. He didn't look very bright.

I introduced the knight, who smiled tentatively.

'Boyo, it's a long way up here!' I couldn't believe he'd actually called Cubby 'boyo'! Cubby grinned. As an opening gambit, the knight had chosen well and it looked as if it might just be OK. I needed to get Ian away and leave them together. An inspection of

101

new cabins, deckhouse and all the bits his money had helped pay for seemed perfect, and after I'd patiently shown him round he left us to it.

Our Welsh saviour asked for a copy of the *Daily Mail* so he could do the crossword and tucked himself into the corner of the mess. Cubby fired her up and quietly, with no one watching, *Monaco* slipped away from the quay. As I coiled up the ropes and tucked them safely away at the stern, *Monaco* began her journey north in the dying early May sunlight. A heavy thud somewhere further for'ard reminded me not everything was fixed for the sea; we still had so many bits to finish. But we were off. The grey houses of Troon slipped away astern. As Cubby remarked, 'It's been a hell of a four months,' but a shiver of excitement raced through me. It was five years since my father had first introduced me to Scotland on that momentous trip to St Kilda. It felt like a lifetime ago but really we were only now at the beginning – even if we did have an incontinent Welshman on board to make things legal. It seemed all he wanted was a beer and the paper, no nonsense about being in charge. That would please Cubby.

'Here you are! I never thought I'd find you in a bar!' Kate teased our diminutive Welsh captain, a month later. He was still with us and whenever *Monaco* tied up, he'd be up the ladder and away to the nearest pub. Although our cheery master mariner was incontinent – he now had four pairs of trousers – he was no bother, and he kept us legal. But it couldn't go on. Oban was a talkative port and what was rapidly becoming known as 'the *Monaco* Lift' amused the locals. Kate and I only had to walk into the pub and he'd wobble off the bar stool, swaying gently, hands on hips. We would each loop an arm through one of his and lift him, legs dangling, bringing him back on board to ensure we were not flouting the Department's instructions.

Potts had absolutely refused to explain and gave no reason for his change of mind. Nothing I could say made any difference; he was immoveable.

'No, Mrs Dalton. Mr MacKinnon is not acceptable; he does not have a full licence, only "an exemption", which is not sufficient for *Monaco*.' But now, a month later, it seemed Cubby had a chance: it was agreed he could go to Glasgow the following day and have a test with someone called Captain Paul Grey.

Cubby appeared, sauntering along the pier. I could tell even at a distance that he'd been to the pub – he was full of laughter and grins. He joked with the fish stall fellow and stopped to flirt with the girl in the CalMac ferry ticket office. He didn't sway, not so much whisky as that, but with his test in Glasgow tomorrow, any was too much.

'Hi, Cubby,' I called.

'Well, it's yourself!' Just a bit slurred, not too bad. 'I'm celebratin'. The doctor's signed my health form: it says I drink a wee bit, just socially!'

'Well, that's great.' I sighed and ploughed on. 'We'll need to leave about seven tomorrow morning. That should give us plenty of time to get to Glasgow for a coffee before we meet Captain Grey. I thought we'd stop in Inveraray on the way back for supper. There's a nice restaurant there beside the loch that does great fish.' He always liked an outing and I hoped the bribe of a decent meal would distract him from the test.

After all, it was his life, his livelihood, not mine. He looked at me, tapping the lid of his green tobacco tin. He pulled out a Rizla paper and began teasing out the tobacco. I realised it was hopeless.

'Good morning, can I speak to Captain Grey, please?' I was in the call box by the railway station.

'Good morning, Mrs Dalton. What can I do for you? I think we're meeting shortly,' replied a firm voice with a hint of an Irish accent.

'Yes . . .' I hunted for the right words. 'I'm afraid Mr MacKinnon's not well. I'm so sorry, but he won't be able to come to Glasgow, Captain Grey. Could we try and make another date please?' It had taken so many letters and phone calls to get the Department to agree Cubby could have a test, my exasperation possibly sounded in my voice. A long silence followed.

'Mrs Dalton, would you call this a diplomatic illness?' he asked.

'Yes, I'm afraid it is.'

'Then I suggest we leave Mr MacKinnon's test for the time being until he feels well enough to come to Glasgow.'

Two days later *Monaco* went off again. Captain Incontinent sat on a wodge of newspapers doing the crossword and Cubby was in fine form. He'd won and was back at the wheel. All was fine in his eyes, we had passengers and he was getting away, out amongst the islands to the space he loved. But I knew he also felt guilty. He was being too nice to me: I didn't need endless mugs of coffee or yet another biscuit. He was at his most charming, witty and entertaining. It was only Oban that was a threat, where someone from the

Department might appear unexpectedly: they often did.

We had a successful week, walking and exploring on Skye and once again the *Monaco* was back in Oban, tied up, cruise finished. Our happy passengers had left to catch the train, our Welshman was in the pub and the three of us were sitting in the saloon, mugs in hand, enjoying the end of another completed trip. No one heard the footsteps on deck. A man appeared in the saloon.

'Good morning. I'm Captain Grey from the Department of Transport and I'm here to see Mr MacKinnon.' Cubby, taken by surprise, stood up and slowly stretched out a hand.

'That'll be myself, Captain,' he replied in his rich, soft west coast voice. I took a deep breath. Which way would this go?

'Well, Mr MacKinnon, it's a pleasure to meet you at last. Would you show me round your boat, please? I hear she's quite some machine.' Captain Paul Grey was clearly no fool.

Three hours later they were still in the wheelhouse. Door closed. Kate and I had run out of things to do. We'd stripped the beds, cleaned the cabins, hoovered the saloon, scrubbed the cookers and were standing in the galley, fidgeting. Cubby's tousled head appeared round the door.

'The Captain wants us out of the harbour. Can you do the ropes, please?'

In the Sound of Mull, by Lismore Lighthouse, Captain Grey made us run through everything. It was not long since Potts had given *Monaco* her licence, but

105

Captain Grey was leaving nothing to chance, nothing untried.

Under his alert gaze we pumped up fire hoses, sprayed water on weather-tight door seals, put up emergency window covers, lowered the Zodiac, ran out the anchor and lifted it. He checked everything, from the engine room bilge pumps to the life rafts, the hydrostatic releases and lifebelts, and he made Cubby set course after course, chatting all the while. Everything worked, everything was greased and all was in order.

'Well, Mrs Dalton, all seems to be fine here. I can't find any reason why Mr MacKinnon should not be allowed to skipper your boat. He clearly knows the machinery and he's worked on this coast for years: his qualifications are more than adequate. *Monaco*'s a fine machine and I wish you luck with the venture.'

It all seemed strange but I was certainly not going to ask what was going on and why the Department had changed their minds: I even wondered if Potts had gone off-piste on a whim of his own.

Nine

The first season was nearly over. With Cubby proud of *Monaco* and happily working, we had had passengers virtually every week and as the autumn began, our advertising paid off and groups of scuba divers came to try the new boat on the west coast. Cubby, as ever in yellow oilskins, chatted while Hughie manned the huge BP tanker, poised on the edge of the quay. Diesel pumped and throbbed down the fat pipe snaking along the deck, coursing into *Monaco*'s fuel tanks.

'Good morning down there!' a voice shouted above the noise. The precise voice, with a hint of an Irish lilt sounded out of place in Oban. Captain Grey. It seemed an age since he had approved Cubby as skipper, but here he was again. I wondered if Cubby had heard the call above the tanker's noise. His reaction to authority could result in anything, it just depended on his mood, and our group of divers was due any moment.

'Well, hello there, Captain,' Kate greeted him. 'Will you come on board? The kettle's just boiled.' Welcoming as ever, she quickly set the tone. Cubby shrugged and, pulling the hose out of the tank, guided the clunky steel connector over *Monaco*'s gunwale and up onto the quay while Hughie reeled it in. Determinedly he turned towards the engine room.

'The Captain's having a coffee in the saloon, will you have one too?' Kate shouted after him along the deck. He paused, wiping his hands on a rag and then slowly turned, making his way into the saloon. Spreading a newspaper to prevent his oilskins marking the seat, he sat down as far away from Grey as he could, eyeing him warily.

'Well, it's nice to see you all again,' began Captain Grey. 'I'm just passing through Oban and I thought I'd take a look to see if the *Monaco* was here. I've left the Department now, you know.' He paused, looking round at us. 'I'm no longer in their employ,' he continued. We stared at him, unsure what our reactions should be. He was the Department's top man, their senior inspector, head of the marine investigation section, a hugely important and influential position. Why had he left, I wondered.

'This is a surprise, Captain,' I ventured, thinking if he's here socially it's probably OK, it's not an official visit.

'I'm now representing the families affected by the *Mary Anne* disaster, so we're fighting against the Navy,' he went on. 'You'll have heard how the whole crew was lost. It's possible her fishing gear was snagged by a submarine and she was simply pulled right under.' He paused and I wondered what this had to do with us. Stretching out, he helped himself to a chocolate digestive biscuit; unusually they were arranged neatly on a plate. 'It might interest you to know how it came

108

to be me who tested you, Cubby.' It had always been
'Mr MacKinnon' before. We were all agog. 'It seems
the west coast was not keen on an English red-headed
outsider coming in with a bigger boat.' He looked hard
at Cubby. 'So I decided to come up unannounced, to
see for myself, see what was going on. But I couldn't
fault you. I had no reason to fail you. You know how
to handle your boat and are familiar with these waters;
you've plenty of experience at sea.' He was not flat-
tering Cubby, simply being factual.

I watched Cubby as he studied his mug, twisting
it round in his neat, strong hands. I held my breath.
Eventually he looked up, 'Captain, I thank you. I'm
grateful to you.'

Relief flooded through the saloon, Grey would be
missed at the Department but no doubt the families,
bereft of their menfolk, would benefit from his astute
assessments. The talk flowed as the Captain asked
about life in Oban, boats, ferries and fishing. He was
interested in it all: and now, without the threat of
departmental assessment, Cubby opened up. I could
see they would become friends, if unlikely ones.

'Katie, have we a spare cabin for the Captain on this
trip, do you think? Could you fix it up if the Captain
could join us?' Kate and I were stunned. Grey looked
even more surprised. Cubby, quick to assess a situation
as ever, recognised that getting him on board could be
useful but it would mean best behaviour all round and
no hanky-panky amongst the divers if he were there.
Kate and I left them to it, as there were beds to make
and stores to stow. It would be best if I could find a
galley slave, someone instead of me to help Kate if

Grey were to be with us, leaving me free to chat to him.

The divers came from Wales, coal miners and sparkies, good mates who knew each other well. They were a joyful bunch, singing tunefully about 'the motion of the ocean' as they roped down their bulky gear. Air bottles, weight belts, torches, dive bags bulging with dry suits, masks and fins: all came carefully onto the deck, followed by six large shovels. With everything carefully stowed, *Monaco* set off up the Sound of Mull with Grey at Cubby's side in the wheelhouse. He was clearly revelling in being at sea rather than behind a desk; divers were a new world to him but he knew well enough to keep out of the way.

Our usual practice was to make the first dive a nice easy one so Cubby could judge how able the group was, and check on our wiry Welshmen's dive practices. He needed to know how strongly they finned back to get on board at the end of the dive and how able they were on the ladder when weighed down with all their dive kit. The site was an hour down the Sound, and the tide created patterns in the water round the parts of the wreck that virtually broke the surface, creating little eddies and swirling bubbles. Cubby had to get *Monaco* close up, judging the strength of the wind and drift of the tide which would affect *Monaco* and the divers differently. She needed to be in the right place to drop them off, immediately by the wreck, so they wouldn't have to fin through the water, wasting air before they reached the spot to submerge. He was good at it, loved getting it just right and *Monaco* was a delight with her unusual manoeuvrability.

The divers plopped over the side when he gave the

nod out of the wheelhouse window. One by one stepping through the special gateway cut into *Monaco*'s bulwark, they dropped, shovels in hand, into the clear dark turquoise water. Cubby eased her astern, washing them gently right onto the marker buoy. Grey stood watching from beside the starboard life raft. I hoped he would be impressed. 'What are the shovels for, Amelia?' he asked as I stood on the top of the saloon deckhouse getting ready to hoist the 'divers overboard' flag. 'Captain, I haven't a clue! This wreck is the *Shuna*, quite a newly discovered wreck and I've no idea what they could want shovels for, but you never know with divers, they're a law unto themselves.'

The *Monaco* drew back, moving astern away from the dive area so we had a clear view of their air bubbles. I loved these moments, with time to look around and with the boat tranquil as we simply waited. Tucked into the north side of the Sound, close to the shore, we watched for the divers to start to surface. The white papery trunks of scrubby silver birch trees caught the afternoon sun; the rowan berries were beginning to turn a ruddy orange. Oystercatchers called as they pottered about self-importantly turning over stones at the water's edge, and an occasional nosy seal, whiskers glistening with bubbles, stuck its head up to stare at us with liquid eyes.

A head bobbed up, close to a white sausage-shaped buoy. 'Cubby! Diver up!' I called to the wheelhouse but already the engine note had changed as Cubby, having seen the head sooner than me, put her into gear. *Monaco* began slowly to move towards the wreck. Kate was up in the bow, checking there were no bubbles

111

ahead; it wouldn't do to run someone over. As we neared the wreck, more heads appeared and *Monaco* quietly drifted to a stop beside the first. I leant out over the water, stretching down to take the shovel which the diver pushed up towards me, wondering again what he'd been doing with it under water. Breathing heavily through his regulator, he paused on the bottom rung of the ladder, pulling on a rope which was clipped to his waist. A bulky, lumpy bag was just visible lurking in the water below. Clambering up, rung after rung, he arrived on the deck, and after removing his fins he leant down and heaved up the bag. Water streamed off it, running through the freeing ports, covering the deck with black slime. Coal. One after the other each diver came up with his shovel and bag of coal.

'Well, boys, that'll pay for your trip,' Cubby called down, amused in spite of the mess on his deck. Captain Grey was astonished by it all, he'd never seen anything like it: this really was the sharp end, not office stuff. He'd seen the *Monaco* at work, seen how well Cubby manoeuvred her and how professional Kate and I were on deck. Now we had a useful ally if we needed one and I almost felt sorry to see him go as he waved goodbye from the deck of the ferry next afternoon. His presence had brought out the best in Cubby but we didn't need him around for too long. Time for a shower, the divers needed their tea and the Mishnish with its music, pints and drams was calling.

Clean and cheerful, I joined Kate and Brenda, our new help in the saloon. She was getting on fine although seemed, like Grey, to be slightly surprised by the mix of camaraderie and professionalism.

'Are you really sparkies?' Brenda asked.

'We're not just sparkies, we're Welsh sparkies,' was the proud response.

'Aye, well, I've wee job for you, then.' This seemed almost cheeky – was she really someone to be giving them jobs, I wondered as she disappeared along the deck making for her cabin? A moment later she reappeared, clutching a washbag bulging with lumps, curious pink shapes stuck out of the top. Tipping it up, she emptied the bag onto the saloon table. Eight vibrators, some pink, some black, some with built-in sparkles, rolled out, lolling around on the saloon table.

'None of these damn things works any more! Could you mend them for me, as you say you're sparkies?' I leant against the saloon door, watching as little screwdrivers and toolkits appeared; heads bent over the vibrators, completely unfazed, they set about taking them apart. Brenda must be quite a girl to have brought so many with her just for a weekend.

'Have you found the problem with that one?' someone asked.

'I reckon I've fixed this one.'

By the time they'd finished their tea, pink, black and sparkly vibrators jiggled and jumped, writhing and wiggling across the table. A burly fellow picked one up. 'You won't be needing one of these tonight,' he growled and winked at her.

Grey had not seen all aspects of life on board.

Ten

The *Monaco* weaved her way between the anchored yachts, creeping into the small harbour in the soft grey mid-summer night. It seemed still and safe after the swells of the open Atlantic beyond the Hebrides and around St Kilda. We were approaching Cubby's second favourite island. (Nothing of course could beat Jura where he was born and where 'the sun always shone'. 'There you are! Just take a peek!' was his standard comment, pointing to the south where the Paps of Jura would be bathed in sunshine.)

He was annoyed because the yachts didn't need to be just there. Anchored between the churches, they could be further in, leaving the deeper water for *Monaco*. But the yachty 'bible' said to anchor between the two churches and in his eyes August was 'the silly season', full of part-time yachties. There would be a few puffins still out on the stac on the south side and the walking was perfect. Our passengers always loved a leg stretch here, enjoying the island's many charms from corncrakes to roses.

A whiff of frying bacon greeted me as I came on deck

and I stuck my head into the saloon next morning; twelve happy-looking passengers were tucking into one of Kate's generous breakfasts. The sun blazed down and after three glorious days at St Kilda everyone else was in a sunny mood.

'Good morning, everyone. I hope you all slept well. Cubby says we'll be here overnight so lots of time to explore and Kate will be happy to fix you up with a sandwich to eat ashore if you wish. Then we'll continue to the Sound of Mull, with a final stop in Tobermory en route.' I could feel Kate grinning behind me; we all loved an excuse to stop in Tobermory: the pub was the hub of the west coast, there was always fun to be had and fishermen to flirt with.

A soft breath tickled my ear, 'I'm off to get my tatties, do you want to come?' Cubby quietly whispered behind me.

'Tatties! There's plenty on board, what do you want more for?'

'Och, those're not real tatties! They're for the passengers!' was the scornful answer. 'You know the Small Isles grow the best tatties in the world? Golden Wonders!'

I agreed with alacrity. There was no mobile coverage in the harbour and I needed to see if there were any new bookings. Besides, a stroll ashore together was always entertaining. Cubby rarely left *Monaco* while she was at anchor, so it meant he wanted a walk too. We always bumped into someone he'd known for years and the *craic* would start.

We sauntered along in sunny warmth, sea on one side as we passed the little church, where tombstones hairy with lichen leant precariously towards the clutch of low stone buildings huddled on the shoreline at the inner end of the harbour. Oystercatchers like bustling waiters worked along the high-water mark, checking under the stones and chattering to each other. We passed the white gate by the entrance to the drive. It was propped open and the track disappeared into a little copse of wind-shaped oak and rowan trees leading to the Campbells' house calmly gazing over the trees across the harbour. I remembered my first visit and that little kiss in the dusk. Cubby, looking at me, winked and held out his hand; large and calloused, it entirely engulfed mine.

'Hello there!' Cubby called towards the byre. Out of the dark doorway came a tall tanned man in his thirties, a broad grin creasing the sunburnt face as he stretched out a hand. He pushed back his cap and scratched his head, revealing a pure white forehead and curly jet-black hair.

'I saw your boaty come in and knew you'd not be long. They're all ready for you over there.' A bulging paper sack leant against the white cobbled wall. 'And who's this then?' Alasdair asked, his deep brown eyes boring into me. The west coast 'look': people didn't just glance at you, they really looked; it was highly effective.

'This is Amelia, you've met her before, she was in the Mishnish that night of the Lifeboat party.' I couldn't remember him either. I could only remember trying not to fall over; it had been a well-fuelled night in a wintry Tobermory. 'Cheers, Alasdair, there's almost no tatties left on board,' Cubby went on. The white potatoes the passengers had were irrelevant and Cubby often cooked his own supper; none of the fancy passenger meals for him. Tatties, gravy and a piece of clootie dumpling cooked by his mother were his favourites at the end of the day.

'Amelia needs to make a wee call, if that's OK, shall I take her down to the wood?'

I looked at him quizzically.

'It's no bother,' Alasdair replied. 'You just take your sack and I'll take her down to the wood.'

The two of them set off side-by-side walking along the shore-side track, blethering and swapping news.

What wood? Why could I not use the farmhouse phone? But I knew better than to interrupt. west coast islanders had old fashioned manners and interrupting would simply be ignored: it was me who wanted a favour. Having passed the church, Cubby repeated his thanks for the potatoes, said goodbye to Alasdair, ending with, 'Give me a whistle when you're done and I'll come and collect you.' In spite of the tattie sack across his shoulders he quickly picked his way over slippery seaweed and boulders towards the Zodiac nodding in the still water.

Alasdair turned inland towards the wood. 'This way to the phone.' He disappeared through a gap in the wall surrounding the little copse. Twigs snapped under his boots as he pushed through the shrubby under-growth deeper into the trees. Further and further he disappeared into the shade while I followed, hesitantly. Stooping, he bent down by a rotting log half hidden amongst the dog's mercury and yellowing bluebell leaves. He fossicked about underneath it.

'Aye, here it is! Will no one put it back where it belongs?' he grumbled, straightening up with a large key in his hand. Pushing on between the trees, he stopped at a small grey hut with a mossy corrugated iron roof and green-painted door. The key turned smoothly.

'Just you make yourself at home, there's a wee chair in here too and if you've a mind there's a magazine or two while you're waiting. When you're done, just lock up and put the key under yon stone.'

The canny islanders had tapped into the phone system: the whole world was a free phone call away. I settled down on the rusty chair and pushed aside a well-thumbed copy of *Playboy*, making space for my notebook. *Monaco* was just visible through the trees so I wondered why I had never noticed the little hut before.

'So here you are, at last!' a voice squeaked down from the Tobermory pier. It was Jimmy, a Tobermory fisherman who had eyes only for Kate.

'Hello there! Aye, we're back again from St Kilda,' she called out of the galley door. 'Come on down; would you like a coffee?'

Although he was just a solid five foot nothing, Jimmy knew better than to jump onto the deck even if it was high water and the distance small. He came purposefully down the ladder and disappeared into the galley. Passengers stood about on deck, keeping out of Cubby's way as he coiled up the ropes, adjusted the big orange ball fenders and put out the springs.

I listed the local attractions, 'We'll be here until two

o'clock when we have to leave the pier for the ferry. The little museum is interesting, over there at the foot of the hill is the Tobermory distillery, there's a great book shop and a few other little shops too. Don't forget to have a quick one in the Mishnish —that's the bright yellow building just there!'

The passengers filed up the ladder, making for the colourful little shops and pubs that lined the harbour.

'Kate,' I asked, 'would you like a hand with the washing up?' Water sloshed noisily about in the stainless-steel sink while Jimmy leant against a cupboard, clutching his mug, grinning.

'No, its fine, thanks, Jimmy's offered to dry up, so you go and have a walk ashore.' He really must have the hots for her if he, a fisherman, was prepared to do the drying up.

When I came back across the pier the passengers were already standing about the deck and the engine was throbbing away. Cubby leant scowling out of the wheelhouse window: it seemed he was in a hurry.

'Am I late?' I asked, knowing perfectly well I wasn't.

'No, you're fine, but I'm told *Hebridean Princess* will be here in a moment and they want our place alongside; we've got to move.'

Jimmy bounced out of the galley door and up onto the pier, ready to throw off the ropes. As I scrambled down the ladder, he growled at me, 'Have you any influence with her? I keep asking her out but I'm not getting anywhere. Maybe you could tell her for me? Just tell her!' He hunted for words. 'Just tell her, it's small but busy!'

Cubby, whiling away the time, as ever was listening

119

to the VHF when I joined him in the wheelhouse. I recognised the voice, Kenny the pier master on the north pier; he was discussing arrangements for the Gun Club dance with Angus, skipper of one of the rapidly diminishing fleet of small clam dredging boats that operated out of Oban. Their 'chain-mail' dredges, which ploughed across the sea bed smashing everything as well as snagging the scallops, were increasingly unpopular, but he had a neat little boat and was president of the local Gun Club.

'Aye, well, it sounds good. You've got a good band fixed,' went on Angus. 'A squeeze box, I hear but not too much of that heedrum hodrum music, I hope.'

'Aye, they're good, so tell the men each of their respectable wives needs to bring the soap flakes,' Kenny said.

As quick as a flash, Cubby pressed the talk button, butting in, without the hint of a smile in his voice. 'Well now! And who's got a respectable wife?' Kenny had never been the brightest and words tended to get muddled.

'Cubby, what are the soap flakes for? I thought the Gun Club dance was a highlight of the year, not a washing party?' I asked.

'They're for the floor. You need a good slippery surface for all that jigging, so all the ladies scatter soap flakes; Lux, mind you, not that new powdery stuff: as you dance it polishes the floor. Shall we go?'

After hearing Cubby was listening, Kenny passed on the news to him. It seemed his father, Old Man MacKinnon, had to appear in front of the Oban magistrates in a couple of days' time. He was eighty-two, didn't have a car and drank what locally was known as 'socially'.

'The old bugger's been caught again! He's been netting red fish!' Cubby couldn't keep the grin out of his voice. 'I'll need to go down and see him, could you run me down when we get in?'

'Of course, my car's at the back of the pier.' I was lucky. Kenny had allocated a special place for the *Flying Tomato*; another little sign I was slowly being accepted into the Oban scene.

With the passengers gone, we moved *Monaco* and tied her alongside Rory's boat. She'd be OK there with no need to move her for a few hours at least.

Rory, unlike most of the men I'd come across on the west coast, had ambition. He hailed from Barra in the Outer Hebrides, one of the islands famous for its seamen, a special race with saltwater in their veins and faraway, horizon-scanning piercing eyes. He also had craggy features and unruly black hair – maybe a Spaniard or two had been washed ashore there from the Armada. They were a swarthy lot. He and Cubby had been mates for years, they both had the Gaelic and blethered over the VHF while passing the time on passage between the islands. I loved listening even if I couldn't understand a word; the cadences had a lilt and a song to them. Rory was Cubby's only real friend, the one person Cubby truly respected.

Rory had worked his way up from small-time trawling for prawns in the Minch to become skipper of a smart newly built steel boat. Unique on the west coast, she consisted of eight water tanks – viviers – and Rory's job was to call at the fish farms dotted amongst

121

the sheltered lochs and collect the grown farmed salmon for processing. With saltwater constantly flowing through the tanks, they remained in prime condition during the transfer. We often tied up outside him against the pier in Oban, as *Monaco* was smaller. As I clambered over *Monaco*'s gunwale on the way to get my car, I noticed all the tanks were empty, no fish, no water and Rory, in the ubiquitous yellow oilskins, directed a powerful jet from the hose into the second tank on the starboard side: the stink of stale fish hung like a blanket over the decks.

'Hi, Rory, have you got a problem?'

'Hello there. It was real bad round Ardnamurchan with a hoor of a swell and the damned fish were seasick; the tanks need a real good clean.'

'Oh, come on, Rory! Salmon seasick! I know I'm English and a girl, but even I am not going to fall for that one!'

'No, no, you're wrong. When the swell's that bad the motion gets going in the tanks, the poor wee fish get sloshed from side to side, they get real seasick trying to keep themselves straight. I had to jettison the lot off Mull they were in such bad condition.'

'Well, I learn something every day up here,' I replied. 'We've no one on board till the Natty Trust lot tomorrow afternoon, so if you fancy a cuppa come on over later. I'm taking Cubby down to see his father now, but won't be long.' I was always keen to get the two seamen together; the stories and *craic* were informative and entertaining.

Eleven

In the bright April sunshine, the twenty-seater plane banked sharply, giving me a clear view of the dour cluster of grey buildings below: Stornoway. I'd seen all I needed to know. There, like a bath toy, was a tiny *Monaco*. I wasn't too late; she was not yet out of the water. I glanced at my watch, still a couple of hours before Bill was due in from Aberdeen; I wondered how much he'd had to pay to get the big propeller blade onto the plane. Needs must. It was Monday morning and if we could fix it by Friday and the weather was kind, we'd make it back to Oban in time.

In the course of coming up to Oban from Crinan, Cubby had noticed a vibration. It was the week before Easter, seven days before the start of the season and the first proper work since the winter. After some time in the bay, Colin, our Oban engineer, had agreed one of the blades on *Monaco*'s sophisticated variable pitch propeller was out of alignment. There was no choice —it had to be fixed and that meant getting her out of the water. The Clyde or Stornoway were the only choices as nowhere else on the west coast had a slipway big enough. I had no intention of cancelling the cruise; our passengers had booked for Easter under blue skies and the opportunity to walk on bouncy turf scattered with spring primroses.

The sunshine made little impression against the thin wind. Scraps of paper were pinned like rosettes against the metal mesh of the shipyard gates beyond which *Monaco* was inching up out of the water.

Cubby as usual hung out of the wheelhouse window. Grinning, he blew me a kiss.

'Hullo, you're here at last.' It always sounded as if he'd been counting the hours. 'I've had to sign a piece of paper,' he continued. 'You'd better go and take a wee look, up in the office yonder.' He pointed to the building at the side of the slipway. My heart sank. I could tell he wasn't happy, but whatever it was he was trying to let me down gently.

'Hello there,' I said, walking into the office, 'I'm Amelia. We talked on the phone earlier. Thanks for fitting *Monaco* in. It's really helpful of you to let our engineer do the work. She's a bit of an oddity with her Danish machinery.'

He needed to know I understood what it was about. The huge man uncurled, and standing up behind a battered desk, he held out a grubby hand.

'We're really keen to get the work done as quickly as possible, so as not to miss our Easter passengers. Mr MacKinnon tells me I should see the paper he's signed.'

After a moment's shuffling through his papers, he held out a single sheet. It detailed how any accident in the shipyard, even a dropped spanner on a big toe,

124

would be down to us, our liability. I flipped open my Filofax searching for the phone number.

Tucking myself out of the wind behind the shed, Motorola wedged under my arm, I dialled the insurance company. 'Could I speak to Mr Davies, please? It's Amelia Dalton; I'm calling about the *Monaco*.'

It was the first time we'd had to contact them since the costly tow across the North Sea three years before: would they remember who we were? Would '*Monaco*' send a ripple through their offices? Unlikely — they'd probably forgotten all about us.

'Good afternoon, Mr Davies.' I read the fluttering text out to him, detailing our liabilities. 'I'm hoping to get the work done by Friday, we've a full complement of passengers for Easter,' I went on. 'Yes, Mr MacKinnon is still the skipper. Yes, he had to sign it before the shipyard would pull her up.' I read it through again. 'Yes, Mr MacKinnon is very much aware of the cruise timetable.' He asked me if I felt Cubby had signed it 'under duress'. I paused, wondering. 'Ah, I see, that makes a difference, does it? Yes, of course he was very much "under duress" with our timetable. So you say it's worthless then, we're not responsible for anything. Well, that's just fine, thank you for your help.'

Coming out into the tearing wind, grinning and relieved, I saw Bill had arrived. He stood under the *Monaco* his compact, five foot two stocky body encased in a crisp blue boiler suit: 'Sunday best' for the *Monaco*.

'Hi, Bill! Good to see you, it's really kind of you to come. You look terribly smart!' He grinned, pleased I'd noticed the boiler suit.

'Aye, it's good to get away frae the yard and they've given me a new boiler suit for the trip.'

I thought of Ali's comment I'd once heard in the canteen, 'Well, it'll be all oysters and champagne working for Amelia.'

Monaco appeared to be being eviscerated. Bill patiently explained how the five-foot-long heavy shaft had to come out so the propeller could be dismantled and the bent blade replaced; at his feet on the slip lay the shiny new brass one. The rubber seals, keeping the corrosive salt water out of the mechanics, would be renewed and the rods to turn the blades for forwards or astern reconnected.

To rationalise the costs, while out of the water *Monaco* would be painted, renewing the green and white on the hull, the old antifouling was to be scraped off and a fresh brick-red coat put on. The eroded sacrificial anodes would be replaced, the decks and hull recaulked where necessary. Bill and Cubby worked on the propeller while Kate and I spring-cleaned the cabins. We were lucky it stayed dry and the work went quickly. When the lads clocked off at midday for lunch on Friday, *Monaco*, shiny with her new paint, was ready. High water was at two; she could be back in the water by four and if Cubby put the handle down we could be in Oban in time.

For the hundredth time I looked at my watch. Where were they? Why are they not back from lunch? The slipway was silent. Not a soul about. It was nearly two, the tide would turn shortly and she had to go down on the tide.

126

I made myself wait another fifteen minutes before making for the office. Big Hands the foreman was ensconced behind the scruffy desk. Glancing up casually, he enquired, 'All going well?'

Could he not remember our conversation? Did he not know his workforce had completed the painting the previous afternoon? Did he not know *Monaco* was finished?

'Yes, thanks. A great job. All done now and we're ready to go. Could you please get the lads to put her back in the water?' I tried to keep the irritation out of my voice.

'You're in an awful big hurry!'

'Yes, I'm afraid we are. It's been good getting everything done so quickly, thanks very much. But we've passengers arriving tomorrow in Oban.' He stood up slowly.

'Och well, that'll not be possible. It'll be next week now. They're all away to the sheep. It's the lambing, you know.'

'What do you mean – "away to the sheep"? That's worse than *mañana*!'

'Aye, well, there's nothing that urgent up here.'

'Are you down there? Cubby! Bill!' A muffled 'aye' came from the depths of *Monaco*'s engine room. 'The foreman says all the lads are away to the lambing! There's no one here to get *Monaco* down the slip, and they've no intention of getting her away till next week!'

Cubby's oily engine room bobble hat appeared slowly up the ladder.

'Stornoway!' He said disparagingly. 'Stornoway!

Sheepshaggers! Sheepshaggers, the lot of them! We'll just have to do it ourselves.'

The passengers appeared in dribs and drabs along the quay looking bemused, weaving through the bustle of ferry passengers, purposeful yellow-overalled trawler men and the odd yachty, neat in a navy-blue jersey. They looked down at the *Monaco*. I remembered my first Oban arrival: perhaps they too felt disappointment that she was not a sleek white yacht, but there were photos in our brochure. As always, they were an ill-assorted bunch: a bouncing little Irishwoman in a divided tweed skirt, a pair of straight-backed mid-sixties ladies, a bristling moustachioed little man, clearly ex-army and Penny, a scatty but talented chaotic artist friend from Yorkshire.

April was frequently cold on the west coast, and Easter was not always easy to fill: Penny was my solution. With a gift for watercolour landscapes, she was to teach anyone wanting to have a go while she captured the hills and lochs for an exhibition of her own to be held in Ilkley.

'I get sick as a parrot, I can't possibly come!' she'd protested but I knew the silvery island seascapes would be the perfect material for her exhibition.

'Penny, don't worry, it's a spring cruise: we'll only be amongst the islands – there's lots of shelter and I'll put something about you and the exhibition into the summer brochure,' I'd added as a lure.

Kate's soup and 'pieces' broke the ice as we went south out of the bay. Though *Monaco* was not full there were enough to warrant the dash from Stornoway and I hoped there would be time for me and Cubby to have a walk or two, maybe for me to do some painting. Hugo would be joining us halfway through.

'Good to be here! I assume I'm welcome?' the moustachioed man volunteered.

Moments earlier I had given the safety talk, but he clearly felt the passenger rules didn't apply to him. He had come round the stern and through the crew mess, in spite of being told it was a crew area and only for passengers if invited. Standing behind Cubby in the wheelhouse, he volunteered, 'I've my own yacht, don't you know? No fear of me being sick — too experienced! Looking forward to the fun! What's the forecast, eh?'

'Aye, well now, you've your own yacht, you say! There's a thing. Then you'll not be minding a hash of wind!' Cubby managed to sound polite but I could see him suppressing a grin. 'There'll be a fair breeze tonight and then it's looking good.'

'Yes, yes. She's a fine craft.' He ignored Cubby's reply. 'I keep her on the Solent. Plenty of work with tides down there! Just you let me know when you need a hand. Always ready to give a hand where it's needed.' Having established his credentials, he went back through the mess, leaving a whiff of sickly hair oil mingling with the cigarette smoke.

'What's the rest of 'em like?' Cubby growled, 'I didn't see them all come on board, only those stiff-necked old ducks. More lesbians! Have you found a lesbian magazine for the adverts? There's that many of them coming, with their hairy legs, sensible shoes and chopped-off hair. They're more men than that wee mannie.'

129

'Come on, you love teasing them! Anyway, there's a cheerful little Irishwoman you'll like and watching how Penny captures the islands and sea with her paints is amazing. Are the sea eagles still nesting in Loch Spelve?'

'Aye, they're there in the entrance. Tell the passengers they'll get a good view of that big bundle of a nest on the port side as we go in. And you can tell them too they'll see some big fat herons on the shore, fishing, if they've not all been eaten.'

'What do you mean "eaten"? And herons are never big and fat, they're scrawny and thin!'

'Well, you're right, but right now they'll be big and fat, it's just after Spring tides and they're always fatter then.'

'Cubby, what are you on about? How can the moon and tides make a difference to a heron and who eats them anyway?' I asked incredulously.

'Well, you see, it's the moonlight; they've more time to fish so they get fatter. They're good eating but only after the moon — a wee bit fishy mind, but no bad if you're not too fussy!' It sounded plausible, but the twinkle in his eyes made me wonder if he was teasing me again.

The two arms of Loch Spelve cut deep into the eastern side of Mull and it was a favourite anchorage of his in a storm. Few yachties took on the narrow entrance so there was rarely anyone around. The loch remained a wild spot despite being so close to Oban, and sometimes we heard the whistle of a dog otter. Cubby had insisted at the outset *Monaco* would run off batteries when at anchor. No machinery noises, no

130

hum of a gennie, or persistent throb of a motor was to ruffle the still black waters of our loch anchorages. While enjoying an evening drink on deck, passengers frequently heard the scrunch of deer coming down to eat seaweed on the shore, a rutting stag grunting, the bark of a seal or bubbling call of a curlew up on the hill.

After two days at anchor, with days filled with walking and painting, the early morning sun felt warm on my back as I leant over the stem. Hosing down the anchor chain, I blasted the sticky grey mud from between the links; it splashed off to return to the dark peaty depths in heavy clods. The chain clonked its way on board, and coming up and over the gypsy, it fell noisily into the chain locker below. It was good holding, a tidy place to be in a storm. The passengers stood about on deck, enjoying their post-breakfast coffee in anticipation of another beautiful day. The little Irishwoman, snug in tweed, peered over the side, carefully studying the anchor chain. The chain came out of the waters a solid grey column, more like a rope until the links were revealed by the squirting hose. She straightened up and looked at me, then leant on the gunwale peering again over the side at the chain. She repeated this several times, hopping from foot to foot, watching as the anchor appeared with a huge clod of grey mud stuck between the blades.

'And does the anchor reach right down to the bottom?' she burst out. How did she imagine *Monaco* had remained unmoving in the same spot through the days and nights in spite of the powerful gusts?

'Penny, we're going south, around Mull, through the Torran Rocks towards the Treshnish Isles and Staffa. If there's not too much motion we'll try to land there but more likely it'll be Iona this afternoon. It's a glorious trip but there'll be a bit of swell after yesterday so you might like to take a pill. If you get right up in the bow and ride it like being at the fair, you'll be fine.'

It was a beautiful passage threading through the turbulent tidal floes of the Torran Rocks before the flat shapes of the Treshnish Isles came into view, but I knew it would also be lumpy. As *Monaco* cruised out of Loch Spelve and past Loch Buie, Penny, singing at the top of her voice, was firmly wedged at the stem riding the swells. It was my favourite spot too, sheltered and exhilarating and she'd get a perfect view. Our dapper army officer was not on deck enjoying the sunshine like the others, but sat upright in the saloon, staring fixedly ahead. Penny's paints and open handbag lay next to him on the seat, with glasses, paint brushes and note book poking out of her bag.

'Hi, Kate, how you doing? Cubby says the swell will stop once we're round the corner, so maybe we should do a late lunch?'

'That's fine; no bother. Kettle's just boiled – could you see if the major'd like a cuppa? I'll take this one up to Cubby.' She disappeared along the deck towards the wheelhouse, mugs in one hand.

The major still sat ramrod stiff, staring ahead, but now, beside him on the seat, Penny's handbag overflowed. Lips tightly together he said not a word: rather than lose face and be sick in a bag or over the side he had simply leant sideways and made use of her handbag.

Running the cold water in the galley, I tipped the

contents, sick and all, into the sink; there was a curious clunk. Water rinsed off her glasses, a paint brush and a handkerchief but in amongst it all, clunking round the stainless-steel bowl, were the major's false teeth.

Our non-practising, or as Cubby liked to believe, practising lesbians remained supercilious and disapproving throughout the week. Even Hugo's arrival had not thawed the frost. Their Greek and Latin pupils at Cheltenham Ladies' College must have had a dry time and their parting remarks joined the anchor chain ones in *Monaco*'s log book.

'We did so love the *Canberra*! But this was ... this was very different.'

It was a relief to see them go but at least they had noticed *Monaco* didn't have over two thousand passengers and the sheepshaggers of Stornoway hadn't prevented our start to the season.

Twelve

The empty house echoed with stillness, there was only me. No one there. No Digby. No Hugo, he was away at boarding school. John was working in London. But I couldn't escape all of the time. I had the office to run – and I had marketing to do, adverts to write, cruise details to send to passengers, the ever-daunting VAT returns to complete as well as next year's itinerary to plan and brochure to write.

It took willpower not to give in to the slightest excuse to slide north, back to Scotland, back to the exciting unpredictability of life at sea with Cubby.

I'd met John when I was sixteen and still at school; he was seven years older than me. It took me years to realise he was a loner, preferring his own company, and, most sad of all, that he was not a family man. He buried himself more and more in his work, and during Digby's short life he had been absorbed by work, just joining us for parts of the school holidays. In between the family holidays, while Hugo was at boarding school, Diggers and I had often gone north, and for the three years Kate and Cubby had known him, they had supported both of us. Life on a boat had suited Diggers and they had adored him. But after Digby died I threw myself more and more into life in Scotland: I would have been totally lost without them.

Over the years Cubby taught me about working at sea, whatever the weather, in winter or summer. I'd happily soaked up his knowledge, learning how to throw a rope so it uncurled across the gap, how to row into a gale: from bowlines to buoyage it had all been new to me but he was an expert and I loved learning. In return I'd told him about the wildlife, sea birds, orchids and wild flowers all around him. He revelled in the wildness of the west coast, its space, uninhabited islands, deer, seals and freedom. We'd crawled to the edge of cliffs watching basking sharks below, tickled trout in peaty burns and poached salmon by starlight. His relationship with Diggers was a delight and Digby adored him. Once when anchored amongst the Cullins in Loch Coriusk, he had decided Digby should see the burn turned into a torrent by the overnight rain. In his little red wellies and matching yellow oilskins, sou'wester pulled down tightly, Diggers sat high up on Cubby's shoulders chattering ceaselessly even though he hated the rain. Splodging across the bog, the sphagnum moss was plump under my boots as I tried to catch up whilst Conker snuffled about amongst the seaweed and pebbles. Cubby worked his way along the shore, sure-footedly stepping from boulder to boulder amongst the bladderwrack and seaweed.

Above the thundering water, I heard, 'Well, my lad, and what do you think of that?' They stood watching the peaty brown water cascading into the loch. Digby surveyed the scene from his unusual height

'Cubby, I think it's the wonderfullest waterfall in all the world.'

Cubby's charm, lively wit and sense of the ridiculous were disarming. Kate, less of an outdoor girl, had been happy to stay on board and watch the telly, turning out fortifying stews and bacon butties. These happy memories were so much less painful than the echoes of Digby's presence at home.

By now *Monaco* was becoming increasingly successful, with our National Trust charter, summer cruises and winter scuba diving weekends – she worked steadily and Kate and Cubby enjoyed their local success. We had acquired some light commercial work towing fish cages around the Mull of Kintyre as well as working for the Admiralty surveying coastal waters. Meticulously mapping the rocky shores of the Outer Hebrides with a bunch of boffins on board making notes and observations pushed Cubby's skills, testing his accuracy, but he liked an achievable challenge and Kate enjoyed a flirt with the boffins.

But, in spite of our financial success, I had two major problems and one fed on the other. *Monaco*'s engine had a seemingly untraceable problem and this in turn exacerbated Cubby's reactions to avoid being in Oban or anything else he didn't like. It was becoming increasingly difficult for me to handle this and keep the problems from John and the shareholders.

In spite of her Rolls Royce of an engine sometimes, after throbbing powerfully for hours pushing across the seas, it would fade. It never stopped completely, but suddenly, unpredictably, there would be barely any power, she would slowly lose way and start to drift. It was terrifying, there seemed to be no pattern and it was completely undermining. On a lee shore or near the stacs at St Kilda, with or without passengers, she would suddenly lose power. We couldn't find the reason and not surprisingly it affected Cubby. I organised the top man to come over from the makers, Burmeister & Wein based in Denmark, but during the three intensive and expensive weeks he was on board the engine had never faltered. Bill and Ali, our engineer gurus in Peterhead, said it was fuel starvation and next time we were in Peterhead sight glass sections should be fitted into the fuel pipes so we would see that the pink diesel was being pumped into the 'day' tank where it fell down to the engine by gravity. In the meantime, Colin, our guru in Oban, had fitted a Heath-Robinson style collection of plastic coca cola bottles to let the air escape. It had worked superbly and *Monaco* had made it through until the end of the cruise season without a falter.

But it wouldn't do for the long term. We needed to know where the air came from so now, on a golden October morning, enfolded by Highland peaks, *Monaco* chugged gently along the pine-tree shrouded reaches of the Caledonian Canal. Rising up through Neptune's Staircase, it had been warm in the locks and there was nothing to worry about – no weather, no rocks, no lee shores, no passengers. If the engine stopped it wouldn't matter. We were going to Peterhead to get the Stickers gurus to put it right.

'You'll have to hurry!' said the lock-keeper as he

stretched up, passing a dram to Cubby who leant as ever, grinning, out of the wheelhouse window. 'They're starting to drain the water, so the reach'll soon be dry.'

'What? Drain the water! Does the Water Board start to empty the canal while there are boats moving?' Cubby asked incredulously. With no water to sit in and float on *Monaco* would simply fall over. From my trusty Motorola, I rang the next lock-keeper.

'This is the *Monaco*! Good morning!' I said impatiently. 'We're at Laggan locks. Do you think you could stop draining the reach? It would be really helpful if we could get through into Loch Oich before you drain out any more water!' I tried to sound polite.

The lock gates swung open, scrunching back against the wet slimy wall, and *Monaco* pushed through the gap, heading as quickly as the depth allowed along the reach, pushing on north. Surprisingly, round the corner appeared a dainty white yacht. Cubby, polite seaman as ever, gently eased *Monaco* over to the side to let her past, red-to-red even in the canal. *Monaco* slid to a complete stop.

We peered over the gunwale as the water inexorably slipped away. More and more of the canal stonework began to show followed by a brown muddy strip of canal bank growing wider as we watched. The casual *laissez faire* of the west coast was sometimes just too exasperating. It seemed ridiculous to be stuck in a canal, five feet away from the bank with the prospect of serious damage looming.

'What'll the fuck'll we do?' Kate called from the foredeck.

A man standing on the towpath with a little white

dog on a lead shouted at us. 'Hello there! Just work her back and forth, you'll get her off. Just keep going – back and forth! Don't give up. I used to clean out this section. It's just the mud. Keep going! You'll get her off.'

Backwards, forwards. Backwards, forwards. Cubby worked the propeller and *Monaco* rocked back and forth. Slowly, oh so slowly, she slid into the middle of the canal and with a sigh of relief we waved to the helpful dog-walker and chugged on towards the deeper waters of Loch Oich.

With no more frights, we arrived. It was good to be back in Peterhead in spite of the fuel problem and a massive list of maintenance tasks. Usually they were done in January but it made sense to do it all now. Sitting waiting for high water so *Monaco* could be loaded onto the carriage and pulled onto the slip out of the water, Cubby and I were enjoying golden syrup sandwiches as we went through the list together. Caulk the hull and deck, strip off old antifouling paint and renew, replace the sacrificial anodes, replace the bilge pump impellors, send the life rafts to be serviced, test gas detectors and fire systems and of course everywhere had to be painted from mast tip to keel. In addition to the regular maintenance there were the Department of Transport inspections and with *Monaco* high up out of the water, the inspector could poke and prod every inch of planking on the hull and deck as well as test bilge pumps and safety equipment. We would have to do fire drills, test navigation lights and practice our MOB (man overboard) strategy, but bizarrely not once had any of the inspectors been into the engine room.

There had been no risk of them seeing our Coke-bottle contraption.

It was always a costly time but all three of us enjoyed it. Bill regarded *Monaco* as 'his': he was always the first on board, bouncing lightly onto the deck.

'Well, it's yourselves! Danny, this is Amelia, but you'll remember Cubby and Kate.'

Danny the apprentice carefully spread newspapers on the seat, protection from the greasy blue boiler suits, and Kate appeared with more sandwiches. It felt like a homecoming as we caught up on the news while the tide slowly rose.

'And how's your dad, Cubby?' Bill's Scottish manners were never forgotten even when sitting on a newspaper in a boiler suit.

'Yes, I'm sorry, I forgot to ask – how did the trial go? He was waiting to come up in front of the beaks for netting salmon,' I added, for Bill's benefit.

'Well, the old bugger got off. He was waiting for the trial, but someone didn't like the fish farm in the loch. So they slit open all the netting on the cages, the fish got out and the loch was fair boiling with red fish. Next morning the police turned up with their van filled with his nets and asked him if he would mind netting the loch for them! He's escaped again.' Even whilst waiting to go up the slip, to mention 'salmon' on a boat would be bad luck.

'Danny,' said Bill, turning to his apprentice, 'what'd be the two things you don't get at home very often?'

'He's not old enough,' Kate butted in. 'Don't embarrass the lad, Bill, and he lives with his ma too,' she added, her tone motherly.

'Aye, well, he'll need to learn afore it's too late!' went on Bill. 'The answer, ma boy, is a blow job and a lobster sorbet!' '

'Ye daft thing!' responded Cubby with a grin. 'It's not a lobster *sorbet*, it's lobster thermidor! Have you no idea of the finer things in life, man?'

Out of the water up on the slip it was impossible to live on board. We couldn't use the gennie so had no power to run a tap or turn on a light. We took up residence in our regular time-warp fifties B&B, living on bacon butties, peas and chips in the warmth of the Fisherman's Mission, or drinking tea with the seventy-odd engineers in the Stickers canteen. It was a different world from shooting parties and opera picnics and I loved feeling part of this good-humoured, hard-working community. From the diminutive seventy-year-old plumber, Henry, who suddenly suggested he could organise a central heating system for *Monaco* to run off the engine cooling system, to the god-like harbour master, who controlled the fishing fleet's movements, my life was populated by vibrant and fascinating characters. I had established a good relationship with Bill and the workforce at Stickers, having earned my stripes by working as hard as anyone else through the cold and snow on previous winter maintenance visits. Watching Bill and asking questions had taught me about the machinery and though I was still a girl with a poncy voice, they respected me for turning a Danish trawler into a successful little expedition ship. *Monaco* was a fishing boat with a difference and Bill was proud of her.

Cubby, with no boat to drive or passengers to be responsible for, was on holiday. There was a mass of maintenance he could be doing but he needed a break. Kate spring-cleaned the cabins. So it was left to me to be with Bill and Danny working on the engine. There was no pattern as to why the engine faltered. Each cylinder – there were five – had its own fuel pump which of course wouldn't work properly unless there was fuel to be squirted in to it by the injectors. Bill, short of precise details, decided to remove each injector for cleaning, testing and resetting. My arm ached as I held the torch illuminating cylinder number 2. It was cosily warm in the engine room. The big red diesel engine took days to cool down and it glistened with a sheen of oil as Bill explained about injectors, turbo blowers and the function of the lubricator with its row of little glass tubes. I wanted to understand it all. I needed to learn the intricacies; after all it was a machine, even if a complicated one, and there must be a logical explanation for the problem.

After ten days *Monaco* was at last back in the water, inspections passed, injectors cleaned and tested, so hopefully the problem was solved. In addition, there were sight glasses fitted into three sections of the fuel lines so Cubby could check the pink diesel was flowing along the pipes. She looked smart, her green hull and white superstructure shining with fresh paint – an oddity amongst the fishing fleet I thought, as I waited, standing in the rain outside the door to the canteen.

We were ready to go but there was one last thing to do before we returned to Oban. It was Danny's twenty-first birthday and I felt *Monaco* should mark the occasion. A garish pink Ford Sierra with bunches of balloons painted on the bonnet in lilac and silver came into view. This must be her. I waved and the car drew up by the curb beside me. A boldly dyed blonde slithered out from behind the wheel, sheathed in a skin-tight iridescent green catsuit, and strutted round to the boot. The passenger door flung open and a dumpy leg encased in purple velour reached down to the pavement.

'Hello! I'm so pleased you've arrived,' I said, wishing she'd hurry up. 'They're all waiting inside the canteen, tea break is nearly over. Can we go straight in or do you need a loo or anything?' I'd found her through the Aberdeen *Yellow Pages* and was beginning to think it might not be such a good way to mark Danny's twenty-first after all.

'How far do you want me to go?' she asked, burrowing amongst the plastic bags in the boot. 'Will suspenders be enough or d'you want the full lot off? I brought my ma to keep it all right, just in case ye want me to take all my clothes off.'

I thought of the assembled Baptists in the canteen. No, I did not want her starkers amongst the God-fearing engineers – Bob might have a heart attack.

'Oh no! Suspenders will be fine, no further, thank you,' I replied firmly. 'I've got the chairs into a circle but no one knows why. When we go in I'll point out Danny to you. He's no idea either, so it's all still a surprise.'

She hauled a cumbersome silver ghetto blaster and whip from the boot and followed me, tottering along in her black thigh boots. We picked our way around the pools of oil and diesel on the workshop floor, Ma stumping along in the rear, boredom oozing from every step.

Once the ghetto blaster was plugged into the tea urn's power socket, it began bellowing at the neon-lit men in boiler suits. The catsuit started wiggling and writhing. She squirmed around the circle making her way towards Danny, slowly undoing her iridescent sheath, peeling out one arm and then the other. She pulled Danny into the middle of the circle of watching engineers. The door flung open and in came the boss who propped himself against the wall. Ma was asleep on a chair by the urn. Danny, lanky and blushing, stood solidly beside the writhing blonde in his navy blue boiler suit. Looking him up and down approvingly, she ran her hands down his boiler-suited legs. The tempo slowed. Still writhing, she rubbed herself up and down against him, undoing the boiler suit buttons as she went. Delving inside she caressed his now twenty-one-year-old chest. Slowly she undid a few more of his buttons. Danny was noticeably impressed. Chivalrously he joined in, helping her out of the catsuit top revealing a surprisingly dainty leopard print bra with red nipple tassels. A crack of the whip and off came the bra. I glanced at the boss but he didn't look as if he was going to put an end to the afternoon tea party. There were grins, wolf whistles and shouts.

She cracked the whip again and slithered out of the catsuit legs to reveal a matching leopard-print thong and suspenders. A roar went round the canteen as she threaded the whip through the lace at the edge of the thong. Then she went back to working on Danny.

Stroking his naked chest, she curled down in front of him, pushing down the boiler suit as she stuck her bum up in the air. The boiler suit legs slid down, over his knees and bunched round his ankles. Sexy young Danny was revealed sporting the palest pink, home-knitted, woolly long johns.

I'd earned a few more stripes and I knew we'd never be forgotten. If ever I needed urgent help, I thought, I would only have to ask.

Thirteen

Monaco was back in Oban. Cubby, confident now all had been fixed in Peterhead, when asked by the coastguards to help with a prestigious exercise, enthusiastically agreed. Forsaking the still, empty house, VAT returns and loneliness, I zoomed north in the *Flying Tomato* to join the fun.

Monaco was regarded by the coastguards of Stornoway and Oban as an auxiliary lifeboat. They all knew us well. They always knew where *Monaco* was and what she was doing, not least because of Cubby's irrepressible gossiping on the VHF. His gloriously sexy voice regaled the west coast world with gossip and jokes: almost everyone twirled the dial to tune in when they heard him. Wherever we went whether to pick up tatties or prawns, we had friends on boats, in crofts and on islands. Wherever *Monaco* tied up there'd be someone to catch a rope and come on board for a blether and a bit of dry Dundee cake washed down with nerve jangling Nescafé.

It was a compliment, an affirmation of a professionally run operation, to be asked to take part in this major

146

exercise especially in the potential weather conditions of late November. The exercise would test new software developed for the Search & Rescue teams, which would improve their chances of finding things lost at sea. Objects in the sea react differently to weather, tide and currents. With the new software, when a call for help was received, the type of object, prevailing weather and tidal conditions would be entered into the national computer system. It was hoped the new software would indicate where they should search. They needed three different objects to test its accuracy. *Monaco* was to drift powerless for three hours, a stuffed dummy would be thrown overboard and the third object was a life raft. *Monaco* with no power would be at the mercy of the tidal current and wind: the dummy would be affected by current only and the life raft purely by the wind. We were also to have a casualty needing hospitalisation to be picked up from the deck by one of the rescue helicopters.

With a reporter from the *Oban Times* and our 'casualty', Andy from the Oban Coastguards, on board, *Monaco* headed out across the bay in the star-studded black of mid-November. We were off to the deep waters south-west of Barra Head at the southern end of the Outer Hebrides: seven hours steaming into a glorious winter night, clear and crisp with barely a breath of wind. With no passengers to worry about or feed, we all crammed into the wheelhouse. This was part of what had enraptured me so many years ago: the blether, the *craic*, the ability to find entertainment in the simplest things far removed from a predictable life of social acceptance and correct behaviour.

147

'For Exercise Only. For Exercise Only,' Cubby's liquid voice oozed into the VHF handset. The green glow of the radar screen and little pools of light from the instruments and VHF dials glowed in the dark of the wheelhouse. I cupped a torch in my hand, and a little shaft of light squeezed out between my fingers so he could see the script. Kate appeared in the wheelhouse, while Andy was out on deck ready. *Monaco* calmly waited motionless in the still of the perfect November dawn. Cubby carried on, steadily pacing each word.

'Mayday. Mayday. Mayday. This is *Monaco. Monaco. Monaco.*' My heart gave a little lurch: hearing 'mayday' followed by '*Monaco*', even when I knew it was purely an Exercise, was disconcerting.

Calmly he gave our position, continuing to read, 'It's blowing hard from the sou'west, heavy rain and poor visibility, there's a bugger of a swell.' (Typically, he couldn't resist a little embroidering.) 'We've sustained damage. We've a crew member with a smashed leg. We've lost a lady passenger overboard. We've no power. We're in need of assistance.' Flying through the ether across the whole of the west coast went all the fictional details. Grinning, he released the transmit button and we waited for a response from the Oban coastguards.

A voice burst from the green VHF growling into the wheelhouse, 'I don't know where you're gettin' all this fuckin' weather!' It seemed someone fishing not far away was sceptical of Cubby's description of the flat calm peaceful conditions.

Having reached the designated spot three hours earlier, we had followed our instructions. We had tipped our lady passenger overboard, provocatively dressed in some of Kate's most erotic undies – a peek-a-boo bra, suspenders and fish-net stockings and of course no knickers. The life raft had followed, its inflated roof bright with reflective tape, and *Monaco* had drifted at the whim of wind and tide. But the lack of wind, and still conditions, resulted in all three objects – *Monaco*, the life raft and body – remaining in a tight little group. The body was close to *Monaco*'s port shoulder while the life raft sat serenely a few metres away.

We waited.

In the grey light of dawn, a lumbering Nimrod aircraft, bristling with aerials, flew over *Monaco*. It banked, turned back towards us, dipped its wings in salute and was gone. Next, just above the water, two grey Search & Rescue Sikorsky helicopters clattered up and quartered the sea around us. Three bright green streaks raced across the radar; the cavalry was coming – lifeboats from Barra Head, Port Askaig and Tobermory, each wanting to reach *Monaco* first. As they closed in, doors were pushed back and everyone waved. We knew the crews well, so it felt increasingly like a party in the pale morning sunlight.

The coastguards had suggested I should be the 'casualty' to be winched up off the deck and swung into the hovering chopper. But the thought of dangling over the sea terrified me and I was not leaving the *Monaco*. Besides, I'd probably miss the party.

During the night Cubby and I had made everything ready. The navigation lights high above gave enough light to check all the ropes were secure and fenders tied down: nothing loose to fly about in the downdraught from the chopper. It seemed to hover horribly close to *Monaco*'s mast as I stood waiting, reminding myself not to reach up to grab the winch man as he landed on deck. Andy, strapped into a stretcher, slowly disappeared into the aircraft's welcoming belly.

The other chopper quartering the sea had found the body.

'*Monaco*, *Monaco*. Channel 77.' There was a smile in the voice over the clattering sound of the rotor blades.

'Channel 77,' replied Cubby.

'*Monaco*, we have retrieved the casualty. I expect you'd like the props back before we take her to Glasgow Royal Infirmary?' Moments later the Sikorsky swooped past. And Kate's undies plopped down in a squelchy bundle in the middle of *Monaco*'s deck. The exercise had been pretty useless as a means of predicting the search areas for the rescue services as there was not enough weather, but no one seemed to mind. The debriefing turned into a ten-hour party thanks to the Tobermory lifeboat crew.

In the following dark December days *Monaco* needed work. Without work and company, the long dull winter days engulfed both Kate and Cubby and a blanket of inertia would descend. Dive charters or commercial work, whatever I could find, would do. But worse than the winter malaise, the big red diesel, known for its reliability and power, had again faltered. In spite of Bill's assiduous maintenance in Peterhead there were moments when the sight glasses were just a mass of bubbles, almost empty, no pink pulsing diesel running through the pipes. Sometimes, it seemed a miracle *Monaco* kept moving at all. There was little reason to go to Peterhead again, and Cubby thought Colin with his Oban nous would be able to sort the problem. He had come down and refitted the unlikely Heath Robinson Coke-bottle contraption. It worked, no hiccups, no faltering and Cubby seemed happy, but I worried the Department would find out and of course the west coast gossip worked overtime. Besides, it couldn't be thought of as a permanent solution; we needed to find the root of the problem.

When an offer of light commercial work came, it was a perfect distraction and I jumped at the chance to have some proper winter income, not just the occasional dive group with their love of pubs and pints. Cubby had continuously pestered me to find him this sort of winter work, since it tested his abilities and used the skills he had learnt as a child out on the hill or fishing in all weathers. It also saved him having to answer the same old tourist question: 'What do you do in the winter, Cubby?'

'Fish and fuck and the fishing's poor!' was always the growled reply.

Towing fish cages around the Mull of Kintyre was not a job to play games with. Quite apart from the winter conditions, the tide ran at seven knots in places and *Monaco* would only be able to steam at a maximum of four knots or the whole tow would begin to bury itself and be pulled underwater.

After dropping Hugo back in Malvern from a half-term of distractions and museums again in London, I carried on up the M6, preoccupied with John's news.

'Men of Harlech' marched out of the radio as I joined in – *swift as winter torrents roaring* – that would definitely be no good. I waited for the shipping forecast: without good conditions there'd be no towing.

Malin. Hebrides. South-westerly 4, decreasing 3; becoming variable. Slight or moderate, occasional rain, mainly good.

Sounded 'good' to me. I hoped I'd find all 'good' on arrival at Crinan where *Monaco* was anchored, waiting for the right conditions to collect the cages. Golden Salmon Producers, operators of a major salmon farming enterprise, needed them moving from west to east; as the crow flew it was twenty-three miles but by sea it would be a hundred and forty. We could only tow four at a time and there was a total of sixteen cages to go right around the long peninsula finger of the Mull of Kintyre. *Monaco* had to tow them through the notorious North Channel where the waters were squeezed between Scotland and Ireland, before turning north up Loch Fyne to finish the tow just south of Inveraray. It was potentially a hazardous voyage in winter even with full manoeuvrability.

All the way along this familiar road I wondered how John's unexpected inheritance would affect us. It seemed a distant elderly cousin, whom I remembered from shooting days with his manservant and pristine Land Rover, had surprisingly left John a dilapidated, rain-soaked pile which lurked in the valley below his parents' house. With the pile came rolling acres, rot and tenant farmers. Also a woman. She rented part of the stable block and referred to herself as an 'Artist' – most definitely with a capital 'A'.

'Hi, Cubby, I'm here at last. Hope I've not kept you waiting?'

'No, you're fine. It's good to see you,' I was pleased to hear as he gave me a welcoming kiss. It was nice to feel wanted. 'We're not picking up the first lot until tomorrow morning, and we've got to get the tide right round for the Mull. Come along in. Katie's got the kettle on the go and Donald's here ready too. Mind you don't trip on the ropes.' The deck was covered in thick orange ropes, lying waiting for action. A lingering smell of stale alcohol pervaded the salon: winter. But now there was work to do.

'Will you tell me how you'll do it, please? I need to contact the insurance people cos there'll be trouble if we damage the cages.'

'Aye, well, you're right, but I've a plan for that.' Practical as ever, he'd worked it all out. The cages were to be roped into a line by the owners with the front ropes tied onto an old tractor tyre; *Monaco*'s towing ropes would also tie onto the tyre. The tyre in the middle would not just take the 'snatch' out of the tow providing stretch and flexibility to ease the motion of the winter swell, but would also make a precise point where the responsibilities changed.

On a beautiful cold grey morning, the tiny hamlet of Crinan, nestling under the bracken-clad hills, gazed calmly west towards the Paps of Jura. All was quiet and still, not a breath of wind disturbed the reflections of the yellowing silver birches or the little white lock-keeper's cottage. *Monaco* eased her stern up to the battered fiberglass dinghy; ripples fanned out across the steely water. Cubby, leaving Kate at the wheel,

153

jumped over the rail into the dinghy while I pushed the end of the heavy orange plaited rope as thick as my leg, through the port in the starboard gunwale. He grabbed it, tying it neatly to the tyre lying ready in the bottom of the dinghy. Donald passed over the rope on the port side and Cubby did the same quick neat knot. The knots were Cubby's and that was enough for me but I took a quick photo just in case as he jumped back on board, going quickly up into the wheelhouse where he eased her gently into gear.

Monaco slowly turned her stem, pointing out to the open sea and the Sound of Jura. Down both her sides the ropes, neatly flaked along the deck, began snaking sinuously out through the ports, until she took up the strain and the cages started to twitch. Four round Polar Circles began to move, each one bigger than *Monaco*: she could have sat in the middle without touching the sides of any one of them. Looking like giant children's paddling pools with their black tubes just visible above the water, they began to line up, stretching out astern. The tow was over two hundred metres long. No wonder Cubby had been adamant about how he wanted it set up. Each cage had a diameter of twenty-seven metres, then there were the lengths of ropes tying one cage to another in a line, and finally from the last one stretched the tow rope to the tyre; then our ropes stretched from the tyre to *Monaco*'s stern. Her long 'tail' was so low in the water it was virtually invisible and she had to make her way through some of Britain's most dangerous waters at a maximum speed of four knots. She had to do it successfully four times in the winter weather, taking into account the strong

154

tides round the Mull. We needed a nice calm weather window of thirty-six hours.

Donald came back on watch to relieve Cubby. Standing yawning, he scratched his balls as he glanced idly at the instruments. 'Cubby! We're going backwards! Have you not noticed, Cubby?' Cubby turned quickly and looked at the new GPS which Colin had installed specially, its green numbers shining brightly next to the Navtex. He peered at it, frowning with concentration.

'Well, just look!' bellowed Donald into the confines of the wheelhouse. His tobacco-stained finger jabbed out at the little white box. Cubby studied it attentively, frowning.

'No – how can that be? What's going on?'

Donald bent over the chart table, checking *Monaco*'s position against the figures on the GPS. Kate snorted, no longer able to prevent herself from giggling.

'Aye, aye, it's a dashed queer place this Mull,' Cubby continued conversationally, grinning at Donald. 'It's the hobgoblins, they control the tide! But I reckon they'll let us loose in about twenty minutes and then it'll be seven to eight knots we'll be making.'

Designed for the drag of heavy nets on her stern, *Monaco* was simply made for the job. There was not a scintilla of a hesitation from the engine as she powerfully ploughed her way slowly through the North Channel and up into the sheltered waters of Loch Fyne. Donald, with little responsibility, was fascinated by her machinery and strength, while Kate revelled in being at sea with no passengers to cook for or beds to make. Cubby, when not blethering on the VHF to

Malin Head Coastguards about tatties and the nuances of towing, was at his most charming and entertaining. We did our watches together and then whiled away the off time with our favourite golden syrup sandwiches while he taught me about towing and we debated how fast a trireme could have been rowed.

After the success of the first tow, though sorry to miss the fun, I left them to it and returned down the twists and turns of the A74 to see if John was at home or working in London. I had tried to catch him a couple of times, thinking he'd like to hear how it was going, to know all was well and the income secure. I wanted to tell him about towing through the night, how *Monaco* had gone backwards only to shoot off at double speed when the tide turned, how we'd had to make VHF broadcasts every hour to alert any nearby shipping to be aware of the great invisible tow stretching behind us, but curiously his mobile had always switched to the answerphone.

Fourteen

After an uneventful winter our usual spring cruises had begun. The adverts I had placed several months earlier in assorted glossy magazines had pulled in plenty of bookings and once again *Monaco* was moving amongst the islands. It was always difficult to gauge when to start. April could be cold and there was generally a sharp casterly wind to contend with; not so easy when the majority of anchorages were sheltered from the more frequently westerlies and exposed to easterlies. Cubby and I had planned the itineraries carefully to keep out of the motion and cruise the lochs and sheltered islands that abounded on this convoluted coast.

Now it was June, high summer, and *Monaco* was returning from her second trip to St Kilda for the National Trust – our bread and butter. Once again the engine had faltered, not stopped but it had faltered; Colin's contraption worked, but only to a degree and it was bad news, especially with the majority of a busy season still to come.

I lay on the damp bank, the sun warm on my face as I listened to the swish of the line above my head. Bees buzzed; I dozed off, tired of trying to work it all out.

'Stop it, you silly dog!' Conker's slobbery tongue licked my face, bringing me sharply back to life on the banks of the River Shin. John, encased in waders, rod in hand, stood carefully in the middle of the river casting into a deep peaty pool on the far side; he was a good fisherman and nearly always caught something. I preferred to draw the nodding blue harebells or stroll through the birch trees collecting apricot-scented, golden chanterelle mushrooms for breakfast. We were guests at a lodge a field's distance away, filled with a slightly grumpy salmon fishing party. Everyone was complaining it was too sunny to fish and there was not enough water, but to me it was glorious. Had I not been lost in worries about the engine, Cubby's increasingly unpredictable behaviour and what might account for John's curious absences, it would have been idyllic; Scotland at its best.

'One last cast and then we'll go back to change for dinner,' John called over his shoulder.

'OK. But buck up and catch one! Tomorrow we're going to Oban to see them off, don't forget.' *Monaco* had a prestigious group of Americans, our most expensive charter yet, and I wanted Cubby to see John: it was ages since they'd met and it would do them both good. I hoped it might also remind each of them that working the *Monaco* involved us all, and together.

As we walked along the North Pier, I could see things were not good. Ropes lay about *Monaco*'s deck, uncoiled, untidy fenders lying where they had rolled. She looked unusually ill-kempt and in two hours the Americans would be arriving. John landed heavily on the deck and turned purposefully for mess door at the stern.

Kate's head stuck out of the galley, cutting him off. 'Well, hello there.'

I knew she was surprised, but I had wanted our visit to be a surprise. 'OK,' I said tersely, giving her a cheek a quick kiss. 'Good to see you, but where is he? *Monaco* doesn't look ready to go?'

Whilst Kate chatted to John I went round to the stern.

'Hello, Cubby. How's things?' Silence. Cubby was fast asleep. Tucked into the corner seat he snored away quietly. *Monaco* was a mess; anyone looking down from the pier could see she was in no state for a charter to St Kilda.

I went back to the galley. 'Kate, what do you think? I don't want an argument about the engine or anything else but he's clearly exhausted. I reckon he'd better have a break but we've only a couple of hours. If John could take him down to his mother's, could you stay? I will see if I can find a skipper for the week and I'll come too of course.' I knew she'd not let me down but it was a big ask.

'But I don't want to drive down to Loch Melfort, I'd prefer to get back to the Shin and fish,' John protested.

'What else do you suggest?' I asked. 'The charterers will be here any moment and he'll take it much better from you than from me. Please suggest he takes some time off, he's not been off the boat in months and tell him you'll drive him down to his mother's house. Then go back to the Shin. Kate and I'll get things ready, give the punters lunch and I'll try to find a temporary stand-in, although he's the only person who knows how to run the engine and machinery. I'll try to work out what to do but it would be nice if you could give me a ring later in the day, please?'

'Anyone about?' The fuel tanker was inches from the edge of the pier and there stood Hughie, ready to pass over the big hose to shoot diesel into the tanks. I knew he was booked to fill them each time *Monaco* returned to Oban – it avoided condensation, Cubby had told me. 'How much will you be wanting?' I had absolutely no idea. I'd watched Cubby many times carefully push the five-foot long dipstick into the tanks, wiping it on the way in, as well as out, to make sure no dirt went into the tank, but I'd no idea how to work out the markings he'd made on the stick or how much diesel *Monaco* used.

'Hello, Hughie. Cubby's not here at the moment,' I said, 'so I'm not too sure. What does he usually take after a St Kilda run?'

'Don't you worry, we'll just take it slow, no rush. I can fill her right up so you can be safely on your way.' It was clear Cubby's absence had already been noted.

'Kate, do you think you could get a really nice lunch ready? Maybe some smoked salmon, crab, whatever. We need to distract them as they'll be expecting to set off as soon as they arrive.'

'Aye, no problem. I've ordered fish from Stuart for the trip so I'll go and collect it now. We can always get some more,' she replied, climbing easily onto the pier. Over the previous few months she and Cubby seemed to have had grown further and further apart. She had always said that if his time on board were to

160

come to an end for some reason, hers would not. She had reassured me of that but at the time it had seemed just an idle comment. I had insisted they should be employed individually rather than as a couple, as both did separate jobs with separate responsibilities; it had seemed fair although not the standard practice for couples running boats on the west coast.

With no Cubby, I needed a skipper; but even if I could find someone quickly enough, they would know nothing of *Monaco*'s Danish machinery. Cubby was the only person who'd ever driven *Monaco* and because of our Coke-bottle contraption, no one apart from Colin and Bill had been encouraged into the engine room. While I had always been there for the regular maintenance in Peterhead or whenever work on the engine was needed, I had no idea how it worked; that had been Cubby's job. I loved its incredible strength, its steady purposeful power and I felt sure that whatever was wrong was superficial; we just needed to track down the problem.

Skipper first. I flicked through my Filofax; I'd never needed or thought of needing someone to skipper *Monaco*.

'Hi, how are you? What are you up to?' I tried to sound casual as Donald's lazy voice boomed into the wheelhouse.

'Och, not a lot. And yourself?'

'Donald, Cubby's got a wee problem right now. Do think there's any chance you could take our trip to St Kilda for me? I've a group of Americans arriving any moment.' I tried to keep the desperation out of my voice. 'Kate and I will be on board too.' I wondered

161

how John would like that. I knew he'd been expecting me to go back and join him at the fishing lodge. 'I need someone as quickly as possible and I know you like *Monaco*.' More to the point, I knew he had the qualifications and lived on the outskirts of town. He also liked Kate's cooking.

By now, in spite of being owned by a red-haired poncy English girl, *Monaco* was highly regarded in Oban. She was bigger than the other boats which operated on the west coast and I knew pretty well that any of the locals would jump at the chance to get behind the wheel. Cubby was envied: he had an impressive command, steady work and an annual salary. I knew if Donald were free, he would come. He'd be OK, he'd do. He was cautious but knew the waters, even if he was a bit of an old woman compared with Cubby. Trying to keep the excitement of my unexpected offer out of his voice, he nonchalantly asked what his wages would be and then of course agreed as I knew he would.

Next, I needed Stickers.

'Hi, Ali, how are you? Fine. Is Bill there? I know it's a Saturday but I thought he might be around. Yes, thanks, I'd love his home number.' Tears pricked my lids, and I swallowed hard.

'Hi, Bill. I'm sorry to disturb you on a Saturday. Oh, you are kind, thanks so much. Yes, all OK, but could you tell me how to start the engine?' Without asking why, he slowly went through the steps. 'Right,' I said, trying to convince myself, 'I think I've got it. But what if it doesn't start?' He chuckled down the line.

'Get away with you! She'll start. You just see. She's

a B&W Alpha, not some fancy high revving modern piece of junk.' He sounded quite offended.

I pulled open the heavy engine room door; warm oily air wafted out. Ducking through the opening, I plunged into the cavernous darkness. It felt almost welcoming – my boaty – she'd look after me!

Pausing at the top of the ladder, I tried to remember Bill's careful sequence of instructions. First I needed to fill the air bottles and that meant starting the generator to get the compressor going. I pulled the clunky handle out from under the gennie and locked it onto the shaft, giving it an experimental push. No movement. I tried again. No choice: it's got to go. I could hear Kate chatting through the wooden bulkhead, so the Americans must have arrived, but where, I wondered, was Donald?

Concentrate.

Push. Push. Heave. It moved round slowly and the gennie spluttered into life, I flipped the switch turning on the air compressor. Shakily, I slithered down the ladder to stand beside the six-foot-tall air bottles strapped against the hull, close to the engine. Reaching up, I turned the big wheel on the top, opening the bottle letting in the air from the compressor and the needle slowly began to rise as the air filled the bottle.

Red mark, close the valve.

Back up the ladder to flip the switch and close down the gennie. I pulled the lever on the top and it stopped. Peace, just the burble of distant voices the other side of the bulkhead. OK, so far so good and I thought I could hear Donald too.

I looked at the dials on the engine: beautiful brass

casings surrounded the glass, each with its needle lying at '0'. I re-ran Bill's instructions in my head. Stretching up to the top of the air bottle I again turned the wheel, and thought I could hear a little sigh of air.

I considered the engine. The solid lump of red machinery stretched into the dark. Fifteen-foot long and as tall as me, it lay heavily along *Monaco*'s keel like a dragon asleep in its lair. What would happen if I'd got the air pressure wrong? The dragon glistened with a sheen of oil, powerful and purposeful.

I looked at the red lever, as long as my arm, with a black knob shining on the end. It stood to attention beside my thigh: the starting handle. Holding my breath, I closed my hands round the smooth knob and pulled it hard down towards my feet.

Nothing.

A pause, then a whoosh of air.

Boom!

Boom!

Boom!

Monaco came to life. The solid, regular, purposeful thump of her dragon's heart beat out. I stood grinning. I'd done it. Bill had been right. I never needed to be frightened of doing that again.

After closing the valve on the air bottle, as casually as I could manage, I stepped out of the engine room wiping my hands on a rag, rather hoping someone was watching across the harbour.

'Hi, Donald, it's so good of you to come. Have you got your kit on board? Are we ready for the off?' My knees shook, but only Kate knew that that had been a first. I busied myself on the quay with ropes and fenders, wondering if Donald could remember how to drive her. The Mull and the fish cage tow seemed another world. But a gap appeared between *Monaco*'s side and the quay, and smiling Americans came carefree onto the deck, enjoying the warm afternoon sun and views of Oban bay. Kate gave my arm a little squeeze, handing me a mug of tea and a chocolate digestive. Rather heavily, I sat down on a life raft.

Three hours later the Sound of Mull slipped away astern as *Monaco* headed north-west and the white finger of Ardnamurchan Lighthouse came into sight, pointing skywards in the balmy evening. Donald, happy with his command, waved from the wheelhouse and the passengers strutted about the deck. Good thing it's warm, I thought, looking at the white 'pants' and silk blouses. I had rung John, disturbing his pre-dinner drinks, but it seemed the fishing party only wanted to chat about the river, so no one had really noticed I was not there. I couldn't just leave Kate on her own or Donald with an unknown boat. And of course there was the engine. With no Cubby everything felt different; already I missed him with his wayward charm and quick teasing humour.

After dinner I went to relieve Donald but as I took over in the wheelhouse it seemed strangely empty without Cubby. He and Kate had been the reason for all this, and now here I was, responsible for lives as well as money. *Monaco* gently rolled her way across the Minch in the long golden dusk while the Americans were happily enjoying a dram in the saloon after dinner. Kate had excelled herself, carefully creating a dinner with no red meat, low salt and 'darling, don't even think of carbs at night'. At least the weather is on my side, I mused wearily.

A piercing wail split the calm. A red light flashed on the little black box under the controls for pitch and revs. Flipping up the bottom switch stopped the noise but the red light flashed urgently.

'Kate!' Sticking my head out of the window, I called down to the open galley door. 'Could you come up here a moment, please?' She'd heard the alarm and was already half out of the door.

'What do you think it is?' We studied the box. There was no sign of Donald, just a distant snore drifting up from the cabin below the mess.

'Well, it looks like oil,' she said calmly.

'Oil! Must be important, do you think I can ring Bill at this time? I've got a bit of signal on the mobile.'

'Yep, go on. He thinks you're a star — especially after that bird with the whip! Go on, he won't mind. Give it a go.'

'Hi, Bill, it's me again. I'm so sorry. You don't mind, well, that really is good of you.' My voice wavered, I was close to tears and if he was nice to me I'd lose it. 'What do you mean how much oil have I put in? I haven't put any oil in! We're in the middle of the Minch so I can't tie up. Oh. Right, I see, OK, I'll have a go.'

Kate took the wheel and I went back into the engine room. Standing in the heat next to the pounding dragon, I peered about looking for the big knurled nut. He'd said I would find easily and at least I knew where Cubby kept the funnel. He'd said the nut was on the starboard side, low down, underneath the lubricator. Remembering times in Peterhead, I knew which the

166

lubricator was — the collection of glass tubes, each one showing how much oil was available for its associated cylinder. Well-greased by Cubby, the nut undid easily and with my legs braced against the engine and a fuel tank, I lifted the oil drum. The yellow plastic drum was slippery and it was not easy to keep twenty-five litres of oil steady even when the motion was a gentle sway and roll. Viscous shiny oil glugged into the funnel. It disappeared surprisingly quickly into the thirsty throat of the thumping dragon. *Monaco* had a two-stroke engine: oil was the dragon's life blood. When the drum was empty (Bill had said use the lot if it would go in), I clambered shakily back up the ladder. No urgently flashing light greeted me in the wheelhouse. Kate reached out and flipped the little switch up; another step learnt.

We spent the night peacefully tied up in Loch Maddy, but of course Hughie the pier master appeared in the early morning, enquiring for Cubby. Cubby *was* the *Monaco*: she had never moved without him before and with Donald making the necessary announcement to the coastguards as to where we were going and numbers on board, everyone would know he wasn't on board. I sneaked below to start the engine, not wanting Donald to see the air-release contraption; it would be impossible to explain three Coca-Cola bottles strapped at the end of the engine. But I was confident now in my dragon friend.

'The Boat Girl', as our immaculate Americans had described Kate, was doing a great job. When their requests for no red meat – fish and chicken only – no sugar and, of course, a low-fat, low-salt diet had come through, Kate had blanched. 'What shall I give them? Will they not want any black pudding or haggis?' she'd asked incredulously. But the hunger-inducing sea air had caught them and in the calm waters as *Monaco* weaved between the buoys and low-lying sheep-dotted islands of the Sound of Harris, they happily polished off bacon, fried eggs, black pudding and squares of Lorne sausage, toast and butter, as well as porridge with brown sugar and cream. Kate, headphones firmly stuck in her ears, sang tunefully in the galley as she stowed away the plates and mugs in their neat compartments, ready for the motion, relieved her menus had become considerably easier.

Monaco, with the bright sharp morning sunshine on her stern, began to pitch as she entered the waters of the North Atlantic, big swells lifting her stem: the Atlantic always had movement and power. Her high bow went fifteen foot up in the air on top of a big westerly swell before plunging down into a trough pushing aside curling masses of frothy white bubbles at each plunge. Water streamed from the deck, gushing out through her freeing ports. It was like being at the fair; she was in her element. Up in the wheelhouse, Donald could just make out St Kilda as a tiny smudge on the horizon, now only five hours away. He was enjoying himself. Even though the motion was so totally different from his regular yachty commands, he'd had a good breakfast and maybe, just maybe, he might become permanent skipper. I left him in charge of the wheelhouse. 'Love Is All Around' by Wet Wet Wet blasted out of the CD player. But it felt lonely out here in the open waters without Cubby.

Remembering his practices, I ducked into the engine room, adjusted the temperature control now that our big red dragon was warming up and glanced at the sight glasses. All were solid pink, full of fuel, all was OK. The new Motorola, carefully wedged amongst the cushions in the crew mess, trilled into the morning.

'Bill! How nice of you to ring. Yes, thank you, just fine!' Relief in my voice. 'By the fish market. Yes, of course I'll call you back.'

I visualised him in the fish-whiffy call box strategically placed in the centre of Europe's biggest whitefish port.

'It's so nice to hear you.'

A cacophony of familiar noises crossed the Highlands from Peterhead on the North Sea to *Monaco* in the grey lifting Atlantic. I could hear the cranes clanking as they delved into fish holds pulling out bright blue plastic boxes, crammed with silvery fish and swinging them up onto the quays. Forklift truck engines buzzed as they scurried about like ants, picking up the boxes from the quays and taking them into the market, lining them up by type, ready for the morning auction. The sing-song voice of the auctioneer was just audible as he moved from box to box. Selling. Selling. Selling so fast you had to be a local to understand. Over it all I could hear the throbbing engines of refrigerated trucks, waiting in rows at the back of the market, ready to hurry the cod, hake, turbot and every other bulging-eyed, slithering species away to Billingsgate or Barcelona. Bill knew them all, the skippers of the Peterhead home fleet. From small wooden twenty-footers to vast steel vessels, over a hundred feet long,

169

bristling with aerials and sophisticated gear designed to cope with distant waters, to fish far away to the north amongst the cold and icy chunks of the Arctic: they were all his clients. Low in the water, in the early morning, a steady stream of trawlers would come into the harbour and tie up alongside the quays: Bill would be there, waiting to hear which engines needed attention; which had a problem the Stickers team should fix so they could go out again, go back to scooping up slithering, slippery profits.

'Yes, I know you don't like that contraption of Coke bottles, and nor do I. You want me to clean the gearbox filters when we get to Village Bay?' I protested, 'Bill, I've no idea where they are, or what they look like. Must I really?'

There was no escape. It had to be done, especially as neither of us knew when Cubby had last cleaned them. Bill painstakingly explained how vital they were. *Monaco*'s gears wouldn't work if they were clogged; she'd stop.

'OK,' I said doubtfully. 'Let me repeat that. At the aft end of the engine, on the starboard side, if I kneel on the gearbox facing forward and stretch down with my right hand under the main shaft I should feel two small handles sticking out. Loosen the four nuts on the top and pull out the two units. With a small brush and a basin of diesel, I have to tease out any bits of grit and stuff from between the combs, rinse them and put each one back in the same hole.' I took a deep breath. 'OK, I'll do it tonight in the bay, but please could you give me a ring tomorrow morning? Yes, same time would be great, thank you so much.'

In spite of the motion, I returned to the engine room to take a look while his description was fresh in my head.

We were halfway to St Kilda, three hours out into the lonely, steel grey of the North Atlantic. Fulmars dipped past, wings almost touching the waves, *Monaco* pitched and rolled closer to our goal. The engine room was hot and noisy, but not uncomfortably so; hanging on against the motion, I went slowly down the ladder towards where the filters should be, glancing at the sight glass near the fuel pump as I made my way along the side of the dragon.

Clear.

CLEAR!

No pink diesel. I looked again. A spurt of pink diesel and a mass of bubbles sped through the sight glass. Quickly I looked at the other two. Neither was solid pink.

All had moments when there was no fuel. Clear, nothing. When there was fuel it was alive, dancing with bubbles. I stuck my ear next to the Coke bottles; a puff of air blew my hair across my eyes. They were doing their job.

When the Danish engineer had been on board during two of our winter dive charters, he'd proudly told me how *Monaco*'s engine, when built in the seventies, had been the cutting edge of marine design. Fuel was pumped up into a small tank six feet above the engine, it then fell by gravity down to the engine and no matter how fast she went, twenty-five per cent more fuel than was needed went up into this tank with the excess returning to the main fuel tanks. This constant flow of fuel through the tanks prevented 'down' time, no sludge could accumulate in her tanks; she need never stop fishing.

Forgetting the filters, I sat hunched on the little walkway above the engine by the small excess tank, my legs fizzing with pins and needles; mesmerised, I watched each of the sight glasses in turn. The one in the overflow pipe was the worst. When *Monaco* rolled one way it was a solid pink, when she rolled the other way it was clear, just air; it was empty. Shuffling closer, I stretched up and pulled off the heavy cover, heaving it onto the metal walkway using *Monaco*'s motion to help. I lodged it so it wouldn't crash down on top of the dragon below. I should have waited, but it never crossed my mind. Kneeling up, I pushed my head sideways into the gap between the tank and the engine room roof and peered in. Diesel sloshed from side to side inches from my face, moving in time with the motion. At the far end opposite my face was a dark hole: the mouth of the pipe taking away the excess fuel. With one roll it was covered by fuel, but when *Monaco* rolled the other way the diesel sloshed away, exposing the pipe opening; with the next roll it returned, sloshing back to cover over the hole, thus pushing a 'gobbit' of air down into the pipe.

OK, but that shouldn't matter, I reasoned. The excess fuel was returned into the top of one of *Monaco*'s huge main fuel tanks; all four had air vents, so the 'gobbit' of air in time would just settle out. I studied the spaghetti-like tangle of pipes, following by eye the route of the overflow pipe, but after the sight glass it disappeared into the darkness of the bilges. *Monaco* rolled on, so all was fine, but above the regular heavy throb of the dragon, I could just hear the Coke bottles sighing. I went down the ladder again and flashed my torch into the shadows of the bilges, lighting up the red side of the dragon. Carefully, my eyes followed the overflow pipe as it snaked past water cooling pipes, bilge water pipes and slim hydraulic fluid pipes.

I traced it again. It couldn't do that.

I must have got it wrong. Slowly I traced it for a third time, my eyes following the pipe.

It didn't go back into the top of a tank. It snaked its way down and joined back into the main fuel pipe to mix with the rest of the fuel going straight into the engine.

The longer *Monaco* rolled, the more air bubbles would be pumped directly into the engine. Of course it was only when she rolled that diesel sloshed from side to side in the tank, pushing the air into the pipe. It seemed ironic that it only happened in the summer, when she worked the long passages across the Minch or out to St Kilda when the motion made her roll so the air accumulated, and not in the winter when we did shorter steams in more sheltered waters. We'd spent thousands of pounds employing engineers, Cubby had become increasingly worried about *Monaco*'s safety and I'd been terrified lest the Department found out. It seems all that was needed was to reroute a pipe. I desperately hoped I was right. It seemed far-fetched that I, a girl rather than an engineer, might have cracked the problem after all the 'experts' had failed, but at least it would be easy for Colin to reroute the overflow so we could see.

Coming back into Oban would be another challenge. I wondered if Cubby would be standing on the pier, ready to catch the ropes. I hoped he would. I was longing to see him, to have his reassuring, if demanding, self, back in charge on board.

We'd managed. We'd been lucky with the weather and Donald had been OK, but it all seemed pointless without the *craic*, the wheelhouse blethers and his curiosity. Donald hadn't even looked out of the wheelhouse windows when we cruised around, showing the open-mouthed Americans the jagged stacs of St Kilda: he'd simply driven. Cubby, by contrast, would have been hanging out of the open window, gazing up at the cliffs, asking if I'd ever seen anything so impressive or pointing out a flock of gannets diving away on the horizon and suggesting we should go and have a look. He'd been there over ninety times, but he never lost a moment to marvel and enjoy the grandeur.

If he were not there, what sort of reception would we get? Would we get a decent place alongside? He *was* the *Monaco*.

There were smiles all round as our happy punters said goodbye in Oban. Holding out three one-hundred pound notes, Gerry, the suave leader, stepped into the galley. 'It's been a great ten days,' he drawled. 'We'd never expected anything like it. Those cliffs are awesome. And the food ... you really did a great job,' he continued, turning to Kate, whose eyes widened at the sight of the hundred pound notes. We had pulled it off without our cool Americans having any idea: not once had they realised what thin ice they'd skated on. John should be pleased, but there was still no sign of Cubby and Kate had no idea where he was.

As soon as the mountain of bags had gone, I called John and caught him at last.

'Hello! We're back and they never knew. They've given us each a hundred pounds! I'll go down to Loch Melfort and collect Cubby, then I'm coming home. I need a bath, I feel soaked in diesel.'

I rattled on, full of my delight at having managed to get back to Oban without a hiccup. 'Aren't you pleased?' I asked eventually, exasperated at the lack of response. 'What do you mean – you're not going to be at home?'

I could hardly believe what he was saying.

'You're going to see clients? But you've never seen clients at weekends before. You want me to stay up here — why? I've no need to stay up here! And I want to come home.'

I couldn't understand it. Why did he want me to stay up in Oban?

The second surprise was equally unwelcome. John told me that without any discussion Cubby had lodged a complaint for 'unfair dismissal'; there might have to be an industrial tribunal. Why? Could he really think we didn't want him? How could he do that? Surely he understood Donald was only a stop-gap, just to give him some space and a break? I was utterly deflated and exhausted. I had been longing to tell him about the engine, how I had sat in the engine room and thought I'd worked it out. I'd made a call to Colin as we came up the Sound into Oban. I'd gone over with him what

I reckoned it was, and he was ready to check it out and reroute the pipe.

There didn't seem much point in going home to an empty house. At least here I had Kate's company.

For the remaining two months of the summer season, skippers came and went. All of them loved *Monaco*, but none of them knew anything about her machinery and none of them bothered to be interested or learn. There was no word, no sign of Cubby; it all seemed pointless and dull. I drove up and down the motorway, back and forth between Lancashire and Oban, but I never seemed to coincide with John. He was always on the other side of the Pennines. He was adamant I should stay in Oban ensuring everything ran smoothly or the shareholders would kick up a fuss. I became the one to ensure the weather-tight doors were greased, that the escape hatches opened and closed easily, that the anchor chain ran free. I changed fuel filters and impellors in the electric bilge pumps, I bled and maintained the hydraulics and gennie, and of course there was my now-friendly red dragon of an engine to feed and keep happy.

Every morning at 7.15 on his way to check the needs of the Peterhead fleet and see who needed the Stickers magic, Bill would ring from the call box. 'Fit like?' would be the greeting, typical of Peterhead, and each day he'd have new instructions for me covering another part of *Monaco*'s machinery to clean, oil or check. From lube oil filters to Racon filters, hydraulics to trans motors, I became a wizard with an oily rag and a grease gun.

'Hello!' I'd caught him. John was in his office at last. 'Yes, all fine. Donald's coming back to do the weekend dive charter and Brian will do the one after that. I'll go and collect Hugo for half-term so I don't need to be up here for a month or so. When will you get back from London?'

I listened, amazed. 'What! What do you mean you won't be home for half-term? Where will you be?'

He was spending the weekend in Yorkshire. A dribble of far-fetched unconvincing reasons slid out of the mobile.

'OK, well, if you can't come home, we'll come and join you, that'll be fine. I'll ring the pub and get a room for Hugo too.' Because of Cubby's absence, it was about a month since I'd been over to see how the work on John's inherited house was getting on. We'd employed teams of people, architects, surveyors and landscape designers, to demolish the bits where rain poured through. The whole crumbling edifice was being resurrected.

'What do you mean "there'll be nothing for us to do"? How can there be nothing for us to do?'

How stupid I had been. At last the light began to dawn. No wonder he didn't want me or Hugo around.

I rang James and Fanny and I knew there would not be a moment's hesitation; we'd be welcome there. The moment the *Flying Tomato* scrunched to a halt the heavy oak door was flung open, and a shaft of warm golden light cut across the grey gravel, lifting the November gloom. James and Fanny appeared with welcoming arms.

'Here you are at last!' James gave Hugo's hand a

manly shake, and Fanny hugged me as we were swept into the warmth of the family kitchen. As shareholders, they knew all about *Monaco*, Cubby and the season's work. They also knew about the unexpected inheritance, but not about John's curious excuses.

'*Monaco*'s fine,' I insisted, as if Cubby's absence was no problem. 'I've found some temporary skippers and I'm rather amazed by how helpful everyone in Oban's being.'

'And where is John?' asked James, as ever getting straight to the point.

'Well, he's staying in Yorkshire . . .' I knew it sounded lame. After dinner as the three of us lingered over the port, I told them what I feared.

'Amelia, you've just got to hang on in there. Don't worry, it'll all blow over. He'll soon get bored, affairs rarely last. Ignore the whole thing and he'll come to his senses.'

Fifteen

The phone shattered the quiet of breakfast, not the office line but my mobile, so not a booking enquiry.

'Donald, hello, How's things? You've a problem?'

My heart sank. I listened as he described a lack of power, intimating something was wrong with *Monaco*'s sophisticated propulsion.

'OK, I'll ring up Stickers and call you back.' A couple of hours later the *Flying Tomato* and I were yet again on the A74 heading up to Oban. Ali, I knew, was already working his way across the Highlands from Peterhead; it would take him six different local buses to get there. But he said he needed to come and see.

After a couple of hours testing the machinery in the waters off Lismore Light, he pronounced slipping clutch plates. Whenever he had pushed the handle down like an accelerator in a car, the big red dragon simply revved faster; there was little 'push' through the water. Ali needed *Monaco* up the slip in Peterhead to be entirely sure, so there was no choice: we had to make our way there. It would probably take us four days instead of the usual three-day voyage and, he said, we'd most definitely have to go through the canal. It would not be safe to go around the top. *Monaco* would never make it against the strong tides of the Pentland Firth.

I made the phone calls, full of apologies for cancelling holidays, and hoped, just hoped my offer to our disappointed passengers of a longer trip later in the season would prevent too much ill will.

'Donald, do you think we should get the two black balls ready, just in case?' I knew him well enough to know thinking ahead was not his forte.

'Well, now there's an idea. I've no idea where they are. Katie, do you know?'

'Aye, no problem. They're under the seats in the saloon – ready in case,' was her immediate response. Not for the first time I wondered what I would do without her. Donald had been the official skipper now for over two months and yet he still didn't know where the emergency equipment was stored.

'Hello! How nice to catch you, where are you?' Rather to my surprise, John had answered. 'Oh, still in Yorkshire.'

It was mid-afternoon on a Monday so I wondered why he was not in the office.

'I'm afraid Ali thinks it's something to do with the gearbox; he'll have a proper look when we get to Peterhead. Yes, I know. I'm afraid it will be expensive but she's not safe at the moment so there's no choice. I'll ring when we get to Inverness. The lunchtime shipping forecast said south-westerly up to eight later, so we need to get going. Yes, I know it would be quicker around the top, but Ali said most definitely through the canal, she's not got the power to deal with any weather: sheltered waters only.'

We left, going north for the canal, *Monaco* steaming slowly up Loch Linnhe, sheltered waters all the way until the very final part beyond the canal exit eastwards towards Rattray Head. She could only do about three knots, but if it hadn't been so worrying it would have been enjoyable. We never went through the canal except in winter but now in the late summer the reaches were scented with the smells of golden meadowsweet, and deep purple splashes of colour from willow herb lining the banks were reflected in the still waters. The canal lock-keepers kept strictly to their working hours, eight to five and a long hour for lunch, but after two days *Monaco* was at the Muirtown sea basin ready to lock out next morning into the Cromarty Firth.

Donald and Kate, both keen on a curry, were insistent we should take the opportunity to catch one in Inverness before the Hobson's choice of fish and chips in Peterhead. Reluctantly I joined them, but I couldn't stop thinking about the forecast. Ali had told me what to do if she really lost power completely. He'd shown me the nuts that would clamp the plates together, locking them so they couldn't slip. All I had to do was go down to where the drive shaft came out at the stern of the red dragon, lie on the engine room floor plates and reach down to the nuts, he said. There were twelve, each the size of my fist, housed in the girdle which encircled the drive shaft. I just had to tighten each nut using the special spanner, thereby locking the plates tightly together. Simple.

The early morning forecast had repeated the late

181

summer gale warning. South-westerly, force eight, soon.

Soon.

If we were lucky we might just make it and a south-westerly would at least give us some shelter. Our passage due east from the Cromarty Firth to where the coast turned south at Rattray Head would be sheltered, providing *Monaco* had power and could stay close in, keeping to the shelter of the coast, but not too close, as it was shallow. The little fishing harbours of Buckie and Macduff where we might have waited out the storm were all too shallow for *Monaco*: she could get into Buckie but only on the top of the tide, so there was no bolthole from the weather once we were out of the canal.

In the open water of the Firth, for the first time ever, I was really frightened. I didn't trust Donald's judgement; Kate had told me that she had been the one to make decisions on some occasions, so I knew she was unhappy too. I desperately needed to replace him but he'd have to do for the moment.

As she moved from the shelter of the Firth, making only three knots, *Monaco* began to roll, a big, slow, speed-sapping roll. I began to feel sick. Was it fear? Fear of what might happen if she lost power altogether? I wasn't at all confident I could manage the nut-tightening procedure even without the roll. Must be the Inverness curry, definitely the curry. The sun shone but the wind was strengthening as I hung over the stern and for the first time in my life was horribly seasick. I timed it with the roll, clear out into the water, not down her side; that would never do. There must be no evidence, I certainly didn't want anyone to know – not even Kate.

In between gale warnings and catching the shipping forecasts I wondered if John was thinking about us. I didn't want yet again only to reach his answerphone; it would be nice if he rang.

Monaco rolled on and eventually, twelve nerve-wracking but uneventful hours later, we rounded Rattray Head to turn south past the Broch for Peterhead. I knew it was bad timing. *Monaco* would arrive off the harbour entrance at about one in the morning. The Peterhead fleet of two hundred fishing boats, steaming out after the weekend break as quickly as possible to get to the fishing grounds, would meet us head on. The weather was deteriorating and we didn't have the power to wait: I called the Peterhead harbour master.

'Peterhead, Peterhead, Peterhead. This is *Monaco*, *Monaco*, *Monaco*.' I twirled the dial to the working channel. Trying to sound relaxed, I went on. 'Hi. Yes, it is an unusual time for us to come round but we need to see Stickers. We've reduced power and manoeuvrability and would like to come in, please.'

A moment later he was back on the channel used by the whole fishing fleet. Calling on the VHF he asked them all to stop and wait, adding, 'We'll just let this wee boaty come in.'

I nearly burst into tears; I really had earned my stripes.

'Amelia, you might as well get a reconditioned gearbox. The whole unit will cost about the same as if we took

183

it all apart, machined the plates and reassembled them. Shall I get onto Denmark and see if they've got the right one?'

Ali's solution sounded sensible but he usually dealt with skippers who, if lucky, could recoup losses like this in one fishing trip with a really good haul or two. It would take us years to get back the thousands of pounds I feared it would cost. The business had been doing well and now into our fifth year John and the other directors had set their sights on expansion. They felt a second boat or a little hotel in Oban to offer our passengers a base before or after their cruise would be good. I'd begged for the hotel, wondering if they had learnt anything about the practicalities of running the *Monaco*. A second boat, a second skipper to find, a second Kate? No, I had put my foot down. A little hotel or nothing. After this it would be nothing. However, we did have the money to pay for a gearbox.

As usual, it made sense to use the time up the slip for maintenance. Bill got going on the annual dragon checking, shipwrights caulked the undersides and deck, anodes and antifouling were renewed and of course her green-and-white paintwork was refreshed.

Weighing in at over a ton, the gearbox had to come from Denmark by ferry and road; it was far too heavy for the flights from Denmark to Aberdeen. A driver would bring it in a van all the way through Germany and France from Esbjerg where the dragon had been made. At seven o'clock each morning I went through the workshop to Ali's office wondering if it had arrived. Metallic clangs and bangs reverberated, echoing about the cavernous work area as men machined new parts, fixed pieces from engines, be they diesel or hydraulic. Many of them knew me and remembered the stripping, whip-wielding blonde. They waved, shouting the usual Peterhead greeting, 'Fit like?'

Eventually, after ten days, there was an oddity. A tall fair man warmed himself at the Calor gas heater, his long legs ended in a pair of pale yellow wooden clogs.

'Ali! It must have arrived! There's a fellow outside in clogs!' I burst excitedly into his office. Empty. He wasn't there; nothing to do but wait. He'd turn up, but I struggled to control my impatience. The door pushed open, letting a blast of oily air unsettle the papers on his desk. Here he was at last!

Instead, a burly fellow stepped into the tiny space and began looking me up and down. 'That your boat? The green 'un on the slip?' he enquired as a greeting.

'Yep, we're waiting for a new gearbox,' I replied.

He went on, 'And how much oil does she use? What revs do you run at?' He reeled off questions. I knew he was trying to catch me out, but the dragon was my friend and I enjoyed answering him, putting him back in his chauvinistic place. At last Ali appeared.

'Ali! It's arrived: the fellow in the clogs must have brought it.'

'Hey. I'm first here,' broke in the fisherman, pushing in front of me at the same time.

'No, you're not,' I replied quickly. 'I was here in the office before you came in; I've been waiting since half past seven, I'm first.'

185

Sneering, he carried on, 'Aye, but I'm a fisherman! I've got to get back to sea! My boat is more important than yours!' This wouldn't do; who knew how long his job would take and I had been here first. Ali was scratching his head, hoping not to get involved in fight between a local skipper and an English girl.

'Well! You carry dead fish! I have live people. Dead fish can wait, mine can't and anyway I was here first!'

Ali grinned.

By afternoon the next day *Monaco* seemed to be hosting the works outing; she was doing her sea trials outside the harbour with a party of the Stickers work-force on board. Ali had given most of the lads time off: I wondered what the aggressive fisherman would think of that. All was perfect, as expected, and after I had written a cheque for fifty thousand pounds she started the voyage back to Oban. I left by bus.

A bus to Aberdeen, train to Edinburgh, a train to Preston and then I supposed a taxi home. I'd been unable to catch John by phone anywhere. Where was he? It seemed a long way home with a probably empty house as an unappealing ending. Digby's bedroom remained untouched; I had yet to find the courage to sort it out. It was still just as it had been the day he died. I knew I must do something about it, but when-ever I opened the door his presence was too tangible in the little room and I couldn't go any further. It almost felt as if he might not be gone. Might one day come back whilst all his toys, games and clothes were just as they had been. The room smelt sweetly of him; there was even his tiny red 'running away' suitcase beside his bed.

'Mummy,' he'd tell me, 'if you're bad I shall run away. Look!' He'd open the suitcase showing me proudly, 'I've got my pocket money and Glow Bug will keep me company and Panda will look after me.'

Sixteen

Next season, Dougie and Andy, both sound trawler men, joined us for a week or two between other jobs and other boats, but they were not tourist-friendly. Dougie mooched about flaunting his white, ageing body in brown Y-fronts. Andy, to override his tinnitus, brought his own CDs, so the decks reverberated to what a passenger referred to as 'booba doop' and, though they had the qualifications enabling *Monaco* to keep working, each had a common objective and thought I was included in their pay package. Each was sure I was panting to join them in the skipper's double bunk. Worse, they put the word around that they'd succeeded. I had swooned in their arms, borne away by passion in the wood panelled cabin in *Monaco*'s curved stern.

Two were 'safe' – one-armed Eddie and careful, entertaining Rory, Cubby's chum. Eddie made me jump when he pushed his one hand between mine as I washed my hands – it's not easy washing one hand. Rory, who now skippered an oil rig safety boat in the North Sea, was a superb seaman. Calm and resourceful, he instructed me to 'flop like a mop' when things got tough and to give his tea 'a wee wind' to stir in the six spoons of sugar.

Running the dragon, the hydraulics and other machinery was a sufficient challenge for me without dodging around the deck avoiding unwanted attentions. They were strong too. Throughout the winter dive charters came and went, and so did the skippers, until finally the crunch point arrived. A particularly pushy one threatened to leave us stranded in the Outer Hebrides unless I provided his entertainment for the night.

It had gone too far. *Monaco* was tied up in Lochboisdale, way across the Minch, and the divers were all in the saloon finishing their tea.

'Kate, what do you think? He's off to the pub; shall we just go and leave him? Will the lads mind?'

'It'll be fine. They don't like him anyway! Let's just go now. Cubby said you're allowed to take a boat to home port, so let's get going. Their tea's finished, you go and start the engine and I'll take her away from the pier.' She sounded confident and the coastguards were accustomed to hearing one of us on the VHF. *Monaco* slipped away from the pier. We did watches and the next morning arrived into Oban quietly with no fuss.

It couldn't go on, though. Something had to change.

My hand shook as I plotted a course out of Oban bay. Easy, I'd done it lots of times while Cubby watched. But this was an uncompromising, pristine chart, not the friendly one I knew well with endless rubbings and pencil scribblings scattered across the depths of the

189

Minch and around the rocky shores of Skye. A waft of sweet perfume enveloped me and a white turban loomed over my shoulder.

When I usually looked at a chart spread on the chart table in *Monaco*'s wheelhouse, it was in a cloud of smoke from a roll-up, gulls crying and a whiff of diesel, not this effete elegance. Through the window, as the silvery River Clyde snaked away into the distance weaving through the tower blocks of Glasgow, I tried to focus my thoughts. I was in the Department of Trade's offices and the turban topped the narrow head of the Chief Examiner of Masters and Mates to the United Kingdom: to my surprise he had turned out to be a suave inscrutable Sikh.

'Two years on watch? Is that the requirement for applying?' I had queried.

'Yes, Mrs Dalton. Let me make it quite clear, that is time actually on watch, time logged in your seaman's book and not simply time spent at sea. Then of course there are the certificates proving your capabilities: Survival at Sea, Firefighting and First Aid.'

Pressing on, with nothing to lose, I had persisted. 'But that means I can never acquire the necessary ticket. To accumulate two years on watch would mean I'd have to be working at sea for about five years!'

I tried to quell the fury in my voice and not shriek. I would not be fobbed off. I reminded the Department that *Monaco* had a grant issued by the Highlands & Islands Development Board and a mortgage from the Clydesdale Bank enabling her to take tourists bringing income to remote islands and distant communities. 'If I were to have the certificates, could I come for a test, please?' I had persisted and so the Department had agreed. In between the weekend dive groups, I had to get the required certificates.

I started with what Cubby would have described as a 'yachty' course and could hear his whispered comments whirling around my head: 'If you're wanting to reach a harbour, say across the Minch, then plot your course to either north or south, then if you're a wee bit out you know exactly which way to turn, rather than reach the shore and start wondering where you are.' His advice was learnt from years of practical seamanship. My tutors were not so keen, but I knew wind or swell could easily put you 'out' by a bit and I knew whose advice I would follow.

'Lights and Shapes' are the same throughout the world and the swift changing of the pressure systems off the west coast were a more-than-adequate training for me to cope with the weather section. But I still needed the certificates for safety at sea, first aid and finally firefighting, and I wanted them as quickly as possible; the prospect of another season of leering skippers was spur enough.

Shivering in my pink-and-blue floral swimsuit, a cumbersome lifejacket strapped round me, I stood at the bottom of the ladder. It was bone chillingly cold and difficult to see much, and the flashing blue lights, occasionally illuminating the massive square pool, were disorientating. It was supposed to be cold; the North Sea off Aberdeen in February was a cold place and I'd tramped through snow on my way into the Offshore Sea Survival College.

I was the only female, surrounded by tough-looking

men. Each was at least ten years younger than me and all worked on the nearby oil rigs. I shivered again. If I'd known the Sea Survival Course entailed jumping off a high board into a pool with huge waves while disorientated by flashing lights I might not have signed up.

The wave machine thundered on.

We'd been told to wait for the signal before we were to jump. The water needed to reach a fifteen-foot swell.

'Don't you worry, lass, we'll fix the life raft for you,' said a friendly Geordie beside me.

'Thanks, that's really kind, but I need to know how to do it! Hopefully I'll never need to again!' He looked surprised as I turned to follow a pair of hairy muscular legs up the ladder.

It was totally confusing: the sirens, flashing lights and darkness. When I reached the platform I didn't even look at the water below. Remembering what we'd been told – 'Hand over your mouth and nose, hold down the lifejacket, look straight ahead – not down, and step out boldly' – I did.

My breath was knocked out of me as I plunged down into the icy water. I bobbed up and thrashed through the swell but it was difficult to swim or move in the bulky lifejacket.

Where was the 'door'? We'd been told there'd be a rope ladder hanging down under the life raft – 'Use it to get inside.' The raft spun around in the make-believe sea of wind, rain and swell. The ladder banged into my shin and I slithered in, landing like a beached whale on the wet bouncing floor to find I had made it first. One up to Dalton.

Next we learnt how to get across the sea to a distant life raft. This was becoming fun. I was inured to the cold now and barely noticed the flashing blue helicopter lights and sirens. Even the swell felt bouncy not frightening.

Legs, strong and most definitely male pushed up under my arm pits and wrapped around me, ankles crossing over my boobs; my head was in his groin. This was how we were to link up forming a sort of human caterpillar with our arms free to whirl like a paddle steamer; our synchronised swimming quickly took us across the pool to a now upside-down life raft.

Why, I wondered, had I been detailed to try to right it?

The instructions were to get out of the water onto its upside-down 'floor', to stand in the middle, grasp the strap stretching across the bottom and then walk backwards pulling on the strap so it would 'flip' over. And of course, at the last minute duck out of the way so as not to end up underneath.

Easy: the wind blew, but the flashing lights had stopped; it was very dark. I needed to use the wind to help. If I could pull up one side into the wind, it would do the rest. Wishing I had accepted the Geordie's offer, I heaved myself out of the water and scrambled onto the top; that was the worst bit. The wind did the rest and I was sure a hand or four were helping underneath in the darkness. Sea Survival, certificate number one: I'd got it. The lads had been curious as to why I needed it but by now I was entirely accustomed to being an oddity.

I headed south to be an oddity again, to the Fire

Service College in Chorley. At least it was near home and I could have a really decent hot bath instead of the usual meagre B&B puddle.

Firefighting turned out to be equally frightening.

After practising on different types of fires with extinguishers, blankets and using whatever might be to hand, we were taught how to get out of a burning building – from the third floor, with only the remains of a staircase and clad in the full breathing apparatus.

I knew how to scuba dive so a face mask and breathing tank would hold no fear for me, I thought blithely.

Peering through the tiny clouded mask, I clanked up the metal framework staircase to the top of the 'building'. The steel-soled boots were far too big, so heavy and cumbersome, I was frightened I'd trip and fall. It was a long way down.

'OK, your turn. Off you go! There's no one in front of you now.' The instructor at the top gave me a prod and I started to feel my way into the room. Smoke prevented me from seeing, but I could just hear crackling over my hurried breathing.

'Don't lean on the wall – it might be hot. Stretch out and sweep one foot right to left in front of you to check the floor is still there, take one step forwards. Repeat. Sweep your hand up, down the wall at every step. Keep going one step at a time always in the same direction; eventually you'll get out.'

I was out of the room and onto the staircase.

'Check each tread in the same way. Keep close to the wall where the treads will be stronger, less likely to give way.'

I carefully worked my way down two flights and was halfway round the next room as I began to realise I was catching up with the student in front of me. There was definitely heavy breathing ahead above my own clumping footsteps, although I could see no one. This room had obstacles. I manoeuvred around an easy chair, avoided a table before bumping into something hard. Stretching out a gloved hand a voice came out of the gloom, 'Help! Can you fucking help! I'm stuck!'

Through the drifting smoke and my foggy mask, I could make out a similarly clad figure whose top half seemed be flailing around; his bottom half was unmoving. Our wily course-setters had left a bed without a mattress as a trap. The would-be firefighter had stumbled onto the bed and was trapped amongst the springs, he was in leg irons. No pass for him, but I had certificate number two; just one to go.

First aid involved pumping dummies, breathing into a Laerdal mask, finding a pulse on a plastic arm and turning it over to drain out the water.

All I learnt I knew was useful, but I fervently hoped I would never be called upon to use any of it.

With my three certificates it was now the moment of truth. I wanted my skipper's ticket.

I drew the pencil line on the chart. Silence from the Turban. Sweet, Indian scents wafted around. Silence.

'Mrs Dalton, would you like to start again?'

I looked down at the chart. I had plotted my virtual *Monaco* straight onto the rocks; she would have been high and dry below the Lismore lighthouse.

Every time I set about the assigned task, just as I was getting into it, he'd change his mind, asking me to do something different; it was exhausting. I answered his questions on rules of the road, cardinal buoys, radar, wind speed, sea conditions, shipping forecasts and lights.

'And what do two black balls mean, Mrs Dalton?'

I suppressed a grin. 'Not Under Command. You must hoist two black balls to warn other shipping you have no power and are drifting. If you're at anchor it's one black ball.'

Over the past four years *Monaco*'s set of black balls and other emergency shapes had come out regularly but only for departmental inspections, thankfully never in earnest. Now that Colin had rerouted the overflow pipe and the air problem was solved, there had not been the slightest falter or pause from the engine. I felt confident about black balls.

Most detailed of all were his questions about fog: what would I do and what were the necessary warning sounds? 'Find a quiet corner and drop the hook,' had been my immediate response, remembering Cubby doing exactly that even when in his familiar stamping ground just north of Jura.

Five hours later, I flopped into the driving seat of the *Flying Tomato* and reached for the mobile.

'Done it! I've got it!' I shouted ecstatically at Kate. Then I tried John just in case he might be in his office, and surprisingly he was.

'He's given me a Class V with Command Endorsement! Can you hear it?' I scrunched the piece of paper near the mouth piece. 'It was exhausting! He's not bad really, but pretty frightening. I never had a clue how I was getting on but I got eighty-five per cent —not bad, don't you think? What's the news on the tribunal? Has Cubby been in touch? What! That's fantastic, I'm so relieved he's dropped it – did you have to pay him?'

It seemed Cubby had already found employment on another boat. I wondered if I'd ever see him again.

Sunny memories of walks ashore, the flower-filled fields of Canna and long watches en route to St Kilda drifted through my mind. The *Monaco* without Cubby seemed pointless. I knew he would have been so proud of me; he'd have loved the formality of my Class V.

John was still speaking; I came back to the present with a jolt.

'Yes, I'm still here. *What?*'

I listened, holding my breath, incredulous. *Monaco* with all her needs from shareholders to Stickers had blotted out Digby's death; I had had no time to think about him and I had filled the holidays too with amuse-ments and distractions for Hugo. Now, it seemed my world was to fall apart again. John no longer wished to be at home. He intended only to come home when Hugo was there.

Seventeen

I hated leaving him. The grey January afternoon and imposing red-brick buildings of school swallowed him up. I knew Hugo needed to catch up with his friends and I should leave quickly, not prolonging the good-byes.

The *Flying Tomato* dropped down through the tidy streets of Malvern and cruised across the flat river plain, the Malvern Hills behind me and the Pennines ahead. This was a tedious slog at any time and with again the prospect of an empty house ahead, I found I was struggling to hold back the tears as I turned onto the M6. John would be in London or Yorkshire, of course; already the chill and emptiness of the house seemed tangible. Christmas and New Year, staying with James and Fanny, had been a 'proper' family time with Midnight Mass, carols, games in front of the fire and long walks, all fortified by James's generous quantities of wine and Fanny's imaginative food. We had raised a toast to Diggers.

The Grahams were good at family times. Their two girls were Hugo's friends: they got on easily and holidays together had been a happy escape. I punched the button on the dashboard. Crystal Gayle, ready as ever to keep me company, swooned, *'Don't it make my brown eyes blue'*. It suited the turmoil in my mind.

Three hours later, Crystal was still at it and I was still determinedly joining in. The cattle grid at the end of the drive rattled underneath as a new mobile phone brick, lurking beside me on the passenger seat, burst into life. Gravel spurted across the field as the *Tomato* screeched to a halt.

'Good afternoon, the *Monaco*,' I said, consciously putting a smile into my voice.

'Good afternoon,' responded a polite secretarial voice. 'I wonder if you can help me, I am looking for a dive boat for a few days in February.'

I held my breath. Work in the dark and dreary months of February was just what was needed: it would give the machinery a work out, and *Monaco* would be warm and moving.

'Yes, she is available in February, we keep her working all the year round. A long weekend? Just a moment please while I check the diary.' I fluttered the pages of my Filofax wanting to sound as if I did actually need to check. 'Yes, we can do that one. Start in Oban? That's fine.' I quoted a nice low rate, keen to encourage them, and went through the basics, ending with my usual confirmation. 'I'll send a letter with all the details, costs and booking form later today, if you could let me have an address, please? Just the invoice with bank details? Well, if you're sure.' I should have realised then, but I was far too excited at a mid-winter booking to wonder. Without bothering to drive on up to the house I called John's mobile, longing to share the good news of a mid-winter charter. It went straight to his answerphone.

When the cheque arrived bearing the name of a well-known ad agency, I realised I should have charged double.

The 'story' they wanted to tell had to be instantly clear, visually appealing as well as intriguing; there was to be no leaving the sofa to put on the kettle during this ad. In no more than five minutes the message had to be clear: it was that of an entrepreneur establishing a scuba-diving school somewhere inaccessible — St Martins in the Isles of Scilly. He needed a loan. He needed a friendly bank. There were to be shots of the bank's rep, inappropriately dressed in a City suit and tie leaving London by sleeper. Next, in a now much-crumpled suit, he was to take the ferry out to the island archipelago. In bright sunshine as the silvery spray soaked his suit, nothing daunted, he was to continue his arduous journey to meet the entrepreneurial businessman on a faraway island. Underwater sequences were to follow as the dive school owner was seen leading his learner-divers through clear blue water with breath-taking scenes of coral encrusted wrecks. As it was a new business, all the divers were to be kitted out in the newest smartest dive gear. All possible due to the attentive support and extraordinarily generous loan terms from the bank.

They had already shot the above water footage at the Scilly Isles, with sequences of the rep clinging unhappily to a little boat as it bounced across the sea to St Martins, but they still needed a couple of minutes' footage of smartly kitted divers underwater with pretty fish swimming past a colourful coral-encrusted wreck. The Scillies, though sunny and awash with daffodils in early February, had proved too windy; the surrounding open waters were too rough for diving the exposed wrecks. But we had the Sound of Mull: we had shelter and *Monaco* had a growing reputation for year-round diving. I had no concerns: we would be able to find them a good wreck dive whatever the weather. There were wooden Armada galleons, Cunard liners or just every day steel cargo ships: there was plenty of choice.

Apart from my not having quoted enough, it was a great opportunity. *Monaco*'s machinery would get a work out; it would warm her through, and it provided me with a perfect way of thanking our regular divers.

'Hi, Steve, Andy, John. Great to see you all.' My team was squeezed around a table at the Little Chef in Dunbarton. Knives and forks worked on demolishing 'heart attack specials'; mugs of tea washed down beans, hash browns, sausages, bacon, black pudding, eggs and fried bread. Steve was to be the 'entrepreneurial owner'. No matter that he bore no resemblance to the 'entrepreneur' in the Scillies; he would be unrecognisable in full dive kit.

I was worrying whether Duncan, one of our most dreary stand-in winter skippers, would have *Monaco* ready. I had arranged for six sets of matching black-and-yellow Scubapro suits, gloves, weight belts, tanks and torches to be delivered to *Monaco*, but would he check the compressor was running cleanly with a new charcoal filter as I'd asked? Compressors for filling the air bottles were notoriously temperamental and it had been at least a month since *Monaco* had been working. I had no worries about Kate. I knew she'd have soup, butties, baps, butter and biscuits ready: she'd be up for the fun and a flirt.

I wished Cubby were around. I really missed him. He would have been in his element, able to demonstrate his skills, joshing the divers and teasing the film crew, but Duncan was humourless and dour. It would be up to me and Kate to make it work — again.

I had organised for the film crew to make the crossing to Mull by ferry and in the dark February evening the streets of Tobermory shone empty and lifeless as *Monaco* came alongside; there were few ferries in the winter so we had the pier to ourselves. I jumped onto the cold, clammy ladder and climbed up to stand by the bollard. Bright orange lights shone down from the roof of the lifeboat shed illuminating greasy puddles. Kate threw me the bow rope and I made a quick bowline in the plaited orange rope as thick as my arm and dropped it over the high pile. After doing the same at the stern, I left the two of them to do the springs. Avoiding the puddles, I crossed the empty pier, making for the steep track that disappeared uphill into the darkness behind the shed. High above, light streamed from the Victorian turret windows of the Western Isles Hotel, which gazed out proprietorially over the bay. As I neared the stone porch, the heavy wooden door swung open.

'It's yourself! Aye, they're here all right.' Malcolm the

manager must have been watching and greeted me with a hint of extra warmth in recognition of the film crew draining his bar in the depths of February. Laughter bubbled into the hall, and I felt suddenly scruffy and dirty, immediately wishing I'd put on something smarter.

'Hello there!' A neat, tweed-clad fellow in his mid-twenties bounced into the hall and came towards me, hand outstretched. 'You must be Amelia. I'm Charles, the producer.' He was just a smidgeon over five foot and not at all what I'd anticipated from our phone conversations. He was embracing Scotland: tweeds, brogues and a whiff of whisky. He was playing his part. A tall girl, a pelmet skirt just covering her bum, martini glass in hand, floated across the polished floor and flung an arm round his shoulders, easing the weight off her pin-thin heels.

'Darling! Where is our yacht? You know I only came all the way up cos you promised me a yacht!' Her extra two foot swayed over him. 'Well, maybe just a teensy-weensy bit to be with you. But you did promise me we'd have our own yacht for the weekend.'

I thought of the sturdy *Monaco* lying quietly at the pier below. My intuition had been right; the Western Isles Hotel with its Victorian pastiche of tartan carpets, silver candlesticks and the odd stag's head were just what Tweed and Heels had envisaged.

'If you come over to the window you can see the *Monaco* down below in the harbour.'

I dragged apart the heavy plaid curtains in the turret window. There was *Monaco*, bathed in sickly neon light, not looking in the least bit like a yacht.

'Oh!' squeaked Heels. A long pause followed. 'I

thought it would be white and shiny, a proper yacht.'
She paused again, considering her options. 'But she
does look big!'

'Darling' smiled happily and the two of them weaved
across the tartan carpet towards the bar.

It was mostly bleary-eyed people who came on
board next morning in the half dark. The only equipment seemed to be one huge camera, almost bigger
than the man who protected it. Clucking people away
like a mother hen, he tenderly bent over it on the
port side of the foredeck. I had recognised his name
from the list as one of the cameramen from David
Attenborough's *Life in the Freezer*, so February in
Scotland shouldn't be a problem for him. Wiry, quiet
and much older than everyone else, he had an air
of calm detachment. Squatting on deck away from
the ropes, hatches and wandering feet, he steadily
checked through his well-used dive gear. Most of it
was patched and the camera seemed to be covered
with strips of gaffer tape. As I coiled up the ropes,
I could hear people below, checking out the cabins;
others wandered round aft to the crew mess. We
were in luck: for February the weather was kind, and
though the dark winter morning had barely opened
up, it was dry with a light breeze from the south-west,
good for diving in the Sound of Mull.

After finishing their explorations of *Monaco*, people
stood about, staring. There were a couple of men with
horn-button duffel coats tightly fastened and a gaggle
of girls in leg-enhancing jeans and cute woolly hats.
Gloves and mittens clutched steaming mugs of coffee.
Kate was on the ball. I worked my way between them

pulling the orange fenders over the gunwales, closing the hatches and checking that nothing could slip through a freeing port to disappear into the dark water as *Monaco* made her way out of the harbour. The low dark shape of Calf Island was just visible to starboard as she headed east up the Sound. I waved up at the wheelhouse at Duncan, but he looked as gloomy as ever.

Kate was in her element. '*I feel it in my fingers, I feel it in my toes*' – Wet Wet Wet leaked out from her headphones as she hummed along, pushing slices of onions into the swirling soup that sloshed around the massive saucepan. It was clamped over the big gas burner, one of the remaining relics of *Monaco*'s Danish identity. Hoping I might cheer up the dour Donald, I went round the stern, pushed up the handle of the steel door into the crew mess and made my way into the wheelhouse, mug of coffee in one hand and a packet of Hobnobs tucked under my arm. Over on the port side, squeezed onto the tiny bench next to the echo sounder, was a good-looking dark-haired man in a dove-grey suede jacket, collar fashionably turned up, his neck swaddled in a tartan scarf. Snuggled against him was another item of arm candy in a blue Barbour jacket, tight jeans and thigh boots. There was just space for the mug next to the compass; I started to make inroads on the biscuit wrapping.

Duncan muttered in my ear, 'There's a problem,' then stopped for dramatic effect. He could always find something to be miserable about.

'And what's that then?' I asked brightly, hoping my cheerfulness might be infectious. Tartan Scarf pounced

205

on the biscuits. Tonelessly and almost conversationally, Duncan went on.

'There's too many people on board. I counted eight
come on board and we've the six divers too, that's
fourteen.' He stopped and looked at me. I breathed
out to get control of myself, silently counting to ten.

'Duncan, why did you leave the pier? If you knew
there were too many people on board why did you
go? Why didn't you say something then?' Tartan
Scarf and Barbour Jacket were listening, staring at us.
This was dangerous. *Monaco* could lose her licence.
Duncan could lose his ticket. Who knew what the
Department might do. Boats like *Monaco* were only
licensed for twelve passengers plus crew and there
were always people watching, people who would love
to have me off the Oban scene. I looked at Tartan
Scarf: he was the director and would know who was
dispensable.

'I'm afraid we'll have to put two of you ashore.
It's a real bore and I'm so sorry but six was always
the limit. Please could you kindly ask two of your
people to be ready to go back to Tobermory in a
moment? I'll take them in the Zodiac now. We've
not gone far and it'll only take a few minutes; I can
catch you up.' His dark eyes looked steadily at me.
He really was very charming, quite my type or any
girl's type really. The silence stretched out. Slowly
he stood up, carefully pulling the scarf closer round
his neck and tucking it into the front of his soft suede
jacket.

'Ducky!' he drawled, 'Don't ask me! I'm purely
Creative!'

Maybe no one had been counting so early on a winter's morning from a window in Tobermory.

'It's all perfect but I just can't shoot without more light, I'm afraid. It's simply too dark! Such a pity as the wreck and site are perfect,' the quietly authoritative cameraman, Colin, told me as we floated above the wreck, a posse of bobbing divers' heads surrounding us, his camera and gear safely stowed on the floor plates of the Zodiac.

He was adamant that he wouldn't use underwater lights: it had to look 'natural'. While I had provided what they had asked for – a dive on a quickly recognisable wreck – I hadn't known the parameters about natural light. Of course it would be dark under water in the weak wintry light of February without additional lighting. There was nothing else for it, Duncan turned *Monaco* slowly back towards Tobermory. The six divers, Kate and I huddled disconsolately in the crew mess.

'Well, that's it then. Now what? Ideas anyone?' I was desperate. I had let the film crew down. They had come up here with high expectations. I needed to find a solution: *Monaco*'s reputation was at stake and as always, we needed the money.

'Let's go and do it all in Malta!' Steve the jovial 'entrepreneur' from Teesside and one of our most regular divers suggested. 'No, I'm serious,' he went on. 'I know the diving there well, there are great wrecks to choose from and the sun will be bright even in February. All we have to do is convince them.' He was a persuasive fellow. Darling, Tartan Scarf and of course Heels loved the idea. Colin the Super Cool Cameraman went with the pay.

Two frantic weeks later, the bright Maltese sun filtered through the grubby terminal windows, as Steve and I stood by the baggage carousel, waiting for it to grind into life. The shots of divers kitting up, getting into the new black-and-yellow gear in the weak Tobermory sun on *Monaco*'s deck had been acceptable. But to ensure continuity the same dive kit had to be used for the underwater shots. Six thousand pounds' worth of excess baggage costs had brought it all to Malta. The agency's budget seemed delightfully flexible. The film crew had arrived the day before and I'd got a limo to swoosh them to one of Malta's marble-halled hotels. Darling, Tartan Scarf (now sporting a chic silk 'pirate' number) plus of course Heels (still in tight jeans but now with white 'fuck-me' boots) were balanced on black leather stools lining the slick chrome bar.

'Amelia! Great to see you! You made it OK!' Charles bounced down from the shiny stool and air-kissed my cheeks. 'It's all good, all good. Come on! We're browsing the optics. We've started here and we are carrying right on down to the end!' Multi-hued bottles stretched along the back of the bar, disappearing into the distance; it would be a long night.

Steve and I had already been in Malta for a couple of days looking for a substitute *Monaco*. But that proved impossible. Instead we had a brightly painted neat little flotilla of wooden boats. They bobbed against the quay waiting. Air bottles were full, weight belts, fins, masks and suits, all were ready. Divers loafed about the quay or stretched out in the sun; no one was in a rush. No tides here in the Med to account for and after all everyone was on an expenses-paid holiday.

Eventually, the minibus appeared, disgorging a rather grey and sickly-looking bunch. Only Colin looked sharp, glancing at the sun, the deep folds of his tanned face softening a fraction in the hint of a smile.

Darling, Fuck-me Boots (now swopped for leggings and gold sandals – she was learning) and Tartan Scarf eyed up the little flotilla.

'We've three of these little boats; the other two are just over there. Colin and his camera can have one, I'll go with the divers in another and you can have the third just for yourselves.'

'Ah. But where's the *Monaco*? Where's our trusty trawler?' moaned Charles. 'I thought she'd be here?' He'd have no wide decks to pace, no cosy wheelhouse for coffee and biscuits, and worst of all no comfortable cabin to sleep off his hangover. *Monaco*'s charms became greater by the moment.

Tartan Scarf gulped. 'Darlings!' he eventually screeched. 'You're not seriously suggesting I go out in that? Charles, daaarling, you know you can manage without me. You know how sick I get and look it's wobbling even now!'

Darling, it seemed, had hidden depths and curiously became deaf.

The little flotilla bobbed out of the harbour and rolling gently in the slight swell. We swayed across the lazy sea making for a cluster of jagged limestone rocks. Even in the February sunshine the sea was a glorious Mediterranean blue and the limestone piercing white.

Tartan Scarf leant over the side feeding the fishes; Darling, now also a sickly pistachio colour, had his gaze firmly fixed on the horizon. Colin coolly checked his camera: the discomfort of both the producer and director were of no concern to him; he would do the same professional job wherever he was, Arctic or Antarctic. Steve had dived many times on a neat little fishing boat which the canny Maltese had sunk specially in a nice shallow spot: it would be a simple, sun-lit dive onto the wreck. Resting upright on the pale sand, she waited below in ten metres of clear water; even from the surface I could see the superstructure.

The lads gently descended to fin around the mast like a May Day dance. They finned smoothly through the hull to pop up one by one from out of the fish hold, rising effortlessly through the hatch and then drifting down like confetti onto the bright sand whilst Colin hung motionless, filming from a distance. It only needed one dive: easy.

The noise of twelve fins slapping onto a marble floor echoed through the lobby: *Slap! Slap! Slap!* Filming all done, Steve and the divers marched in single file through the hotel still fully clad in black-and-yellow dry suits, masks and fins, breathing noisily through snorkels. The gear had to be washed in fresh water before it could be freighted back to Oban and a shower had seemed the simplest solution. The black-and-yellow aliens slapped on towards the lift. Eyes lifted up from knitting, hands paused over chess pieces. Escaping the English winter, the hotel offered a cheap heated alternative to the loneliness of old age and the inhabitants of God's Waiting Room stared in amazement as the divers paraded through the foyer. Over the sound of the tinkling little fountain came a woman's high-pitched voice, ringing with disapproval.

'Oh! That's it. They're *divers* of course! I told you, darling, they weren't ordinary people.'

Eighteen

Would he recognise me, I wondered, as I eased myself to the front of the throng waiting in Arrivals at Glasgow airport. I could remember him quite clearly. His cheerful round little face, the penetrating eyes and soft Irish voice. I was taking a big risk.

Monaco had been at Bangor, in Northern Ireland, following Cubby's idea that a cruise on the colourful Irish coast would be a change and probably a good seller, but that was eighteen months ago and now he was not here. Instead, *Monaco* had Murray. He'd been working at a fish farm when the bush telegraph reached Ullapool that I still hadn't found a permanent skipper; the west coast was hardly a big pond. At the time he had seemed a good find, had the right qualifications and was personable in a dark, hairy, gypsy-like way. Kate seemed to like him too, so I had been optimistic, but it had become increasingly apparent he was lazy. Mysteriously, whenever I appeared, something had always cropped up which had prevented him from doing the maintenance. He was also an arrogant chauvinist enjoying the regular wage, *Monaco*'s position and hard-earned goodwill. He had no idea I thought him useless. Having done the maintenance myself, I could see what had been missed. But I had no choice: the other options were an even less appealing bunch, so Murray had stayed whilst I set about looking further afield.

Sitting to one side, watching a well-oiled Murray loudly hold forth on Scotland and all its glories, I noticed the Irishman. He was watching Murray, and me, as he nursed his pint of Guinness. Boredom and irritation must have shown on my face. Cubby had been right: *Monaco* was full and our passengers were also in the bar. Some looked surprised, possibly wondering if tomorrow's scheduled cruise through the tidal entrance of Strangford Lough would be on. We all knew Murray was unfamiliar with this stretch of coast but he'd boasted loudly over dinner about his ability to work in new places, bragging about how demanding the tidal streams were in the entrance to the Lough. But right now he didn't have the appearance of someone who would be clear-headed in the morning.

My fellow watcher stood up, Guinness in hand. He was small and slightly bowlegged, a little Irish leprechaun, I thought with a smile.

'You could do without that,' he said, nodding his head across the room at the raucous group where Murray held court. I didn't want to discuss him; I had nothing nice to say.

'Is this your part of the world?' I asked, thinking I'd take advantage of his local knowledge.

'Nope, from further south. I'm after coming from Ballymoney.'

'I'm afraid I've no idea where Ballymoney is, but it sounds like a useful place to come from!'

He grinned. 'I saw you come in this afternoon,' he went on. *Monaco* always drew attention. 'I've the blue dive boat across the harbour. You're welcome for a coffee in the morning. I reckon you'll have time.' Again, he nodded his head in the direction of *Monaco*'s skipper. 'There'll be no early start by the look of that lot.'

Next morning, I sauntered round whilst Kate made breakfast for the passengers. I was wondering about his quick assessment of the previous night. Of Murray there was no sign. He clearly had no idea how thin the ice was.

It was five months later and here I was waiting for the leprechaun at Glasgow airport. *Monaco* had a Christmas and New Year charter, a booking John was adamant I should not turn down. RAF divers were good, disciplined and paid immediately, plus it might lead to future groups.

'No!' I had really put my foot down. 'I know I've got the qualifications now but a mid-winter dive charter is tricky and needs a much better boat handler, with more experience than me. Kate is off too, so I'll do the cooking if you insist but I'm not taking on all the responsibilities.'

Murray, by refusing to work over Christmas, had signed his own dismissal and Connor the Irishman had come to mind. I remembered he had told me how he taught at one of the Irish yachting colleges and I knew he had skippered a dive boat for years. To my surprise, he'd agreed and suspiciously I wondered why. He'd never been to the west coast, knew nothing of *Monaco* and he made it quite clear it would be up to me to run the engine, operate the hydraulics and air compressor to fill the divers' bottles and of course do the cooking. He would 'drive'.

The leprechaun appeared at last: flat cap pulled down, he sauntered out of Arrivals. I'd forgotten how small he was.

'Hello, Connor, did you have a good flight?' He grunted and gave a nod. He had seemed easy, chatty and friendly in Bangor, but maybe he was already regretting coming. 'I've booked us into the Travel Lodge near Stirling. Not exactly the Ritz, I know, but it's on the Oban road and we'll need to get going in good time in the morning. There's a lot to get ready. I've asked Hughie to bring the fuel at eight. There's the beds to make up, stores to get and the fresh-water tanks will need filling. I expect the divers'll arrive about three, before it gets dark.'

He said nothing, just looked at me apparently unconcerned; after all, it was just the usual collection of jobs for any charter. After sinking a few pints of McEwans to wash down his supper of flaccid fish and greasy chips at a pub on the outskirts of Stirling, we parted in the bare bright passage of the Little Chef. A miasma of stale pub tobacco smoke hung in the cold air, red-and-green tinsel stars twizzled from bits of Sellotape stuck to the ceiling. It was two days before Christmas; I fought back the tears.

I was too cold to sleep much, so the alarm was almost a relief, but it still seemed like the middle of the

215

night it was so dark. Proper light wouldn't be up for at least four hours; daylight came so late in December. I swung my legs out of bed and pottered across to the grimy window. The oily puddles illuminated by the petrol pumps trembled gently. A steady drenching drizzle hung in curtains across the forecourt; a proper downpour would have been preferable, as they usually ended more quickly. I dressed quickly in layers, lots of them.

Across the passage, I knocked on his door. Silence. He'd asked me to wake him so I rapped harder, the flimsy door rattling loudly.

'Hello! Hello! It's six o'clock,' I bellowed at the door frame, hoping there'd be some response, hoping he was already awake; too bad if I woke up the whole corridor. What would I do if he didn't get up? 'I'm going to the cafe for some breakfast, see you in a moment,' I said hopefully. Still nothing. Silence. As I raised my hand to try again.

'Fuck off! I'm not coming out to play!'

Disconsolately, sitting in the Little Chef, I gazed out of the grimy window. I had put all my faith in him, and it never occurred to me he'd come over but not do the job. How could I have thought it would work? I knew virtually nothing about him and what did my charter or any of it matter to him? I didn't even notice the gust of cold air, as he came in.

'Tea. Tea would be good.'

Well, at least he was up and ready to go.

Slowly the darkness loosened and the hills became solid lumps darker than the sky by the time I turned the *Flying Tomato* off the motorway north of Stirling.

216

Another hour to Oban but I knew the road well, it was a drive I enjoyed and it was likely the road would be empty. Twisting and turning, we zoomed along the winding lochside making our way up Loch Lubnaig: I knew every corner, every dip, twist and turn. The drizzle had eased and I could make out the stark silhouettes of black winter trees clustered on corners, the hills reflected in the still dark waters of Loch Earn. Connor, in the passenger seat, stared ahead. Again and again I had opened a conversation, trying to think of a topic that would elicit an answer, but had failed to get a response. I gave up. If he didn't find the silence awkward, nor would I.

Fast quick gear changes, down for the bends and up through the range as I accelerated away on the straights. I loved driving my *Tomato* and it was getting lighter now and the clouds had turned a milky pale blue. There were rusty brown patches of bracken and the stark silhouettes were turning into straggly silver birch trees. Eventually, as we crested the rise, Mull, the islands and Oban were spread out before us. I scanned over the roofs across the bay towards the island of Kerrera sheltering the harbour entrance, and there, safely on her mooring, was *Monaco*.

It was always an emotional moment: she looked smart and powerful and now I knew how to operate her she seemed even more welcoming. But it was Christmas. I would be missing everything. In spite of all that needed to be done, my mind slipped away, wrestling with the same problem I'd gone over so many times. If only I could find a reliable, safe skipper I wouldn't need to be stuck up here, stuck away from all the other parts that made up my life. I hoped Hugo would be happy skiing, and indeed that was probably the only certain part: he would definitely enjoy the skiing. But for me, there was the responsibility of the dive charter with a skipper I knew nothing of. It would be exhausting and cold but at least I'd not have to fight him off, I was sure of that.

I brought the *Flying Tomato* to a halt on the North Quay and waved to Gordon, the pier master, through the window of his office. I mustn't forget his Christmas present sitting on the back seat — a thank-you for letting me park on the quay. Connor gave himself a shake. He opened the door stretching his bandy legs onto the tarmac. Easing out of his seat, he slowly stood up, all five foot three of him, and gazed across the harbour towards the *Monaco* and said the first words since 'tea'.

'I hope this fuckin' sea is flatter than this fuckin' country.'

It had never occurred to me he might be carsick.

Monaco did not let me down. I managed to heave round the handle to start the gennie. The compressor pumped air into the two bottles to start the engine. I always ran through my mental list just as Bill had taught me – sight glasses on the lubricator, one for each cylinder – each was full. The filters I knew were clean, as I'd done them before going home after the last charter. When the air-start cylinder was full, I pulled down the heavy black knob of the starter lever. *Poof!* A huge rush of air, a moment's pause, before—

Boom! Boom! Boom! Monaco came alive!

The none-too-generous space between the two fishing boats where Gordon had told us to go would

218

be tight. Typical, I knew he'd done it as a test; it was tempting to ignore him and put her on the end of the pier where there was lots of space. I couldn't even see Connor in the wheelhouse he was so small and he hadn't even wanted to drive her around a bit to get the 'feel' of her, just go straight to the pier. I held my breath: the fenders were out, but I was poised, ready with one of the biggest orange balls, ready to lob it over the side wherever it might be needed. But *Monaco* came in so smooth and slow, she gently slipped alongside and stopped just kissing the quay. I leapt up the ladder, rope slung over my shoulder, tied a bowline and dropped it over the bollard. People crossed the pier, staring down, eager to see who was in the wheelhouse this time.

'Hi, Stuart! All OK with you?'

'Aye, apart from the dark and lack of life! And yourself?'

'Fine, thanks; we've a dive charter for Christmas and New Year. Would you have a salmon and some prawns for me, please? I need something nice for their tea.'

Kate had asked for time off and it seemed unfair to insist she came; I knew I could manage the food and I was beginning to think Connor might not be such a bad bet after all.

He appeared out of the mess door.

'This is Connor. He's over from Ireland for the charter.'

'Well, you're welcome here and if you've a mind for a bite I'm cooking today.'

'Fantastic, we'll be there! We're not leaving until

later.' I turned to Connor. 'Stuart is a great cook, all from his caravan over there at the end of the pier. He's a wizard with garlic, wine and prawns — he's even made it into the *Michelin Guide*!' Did Connor have any idea of the *Michelin Guide*?

Hughie's BP tanker nosed onto the pier.

'Hi, Hughie, how's things?' They felt like real friends and I knew the midwinter business would be welcome. Soon the fat hose coiled along the deck, throbbing as it pumped diesel into *Monaco*'s tanks.

Land Rovers appeared next, disgorging cumbersome bags of dive kit. Air bottles, dry suits came down, heavy weight belts were carefully lodged in the blue plastic fish box lashed beside the open hatch: they knew the form well. When everyone was ready, *Monaco*, Connor at the wheel, headed out of Oban bay, her stem pointing west towards the Sound of Mull. I pulled in the fenders, helped by a chopper pilot I knew from the last time they'd been on board. The others were out on deck too, leaning against hatches or the gunwales, all assembling their dive kit, tinkering with screwdrivers, checking neoprene seals and patching bits with gaffer tape. Diving was like boating; preparation was half the fun.

A big red-and-white CalMac ferry appeared in the harbour entrance, and still going full speed she came quickly towards us. Connor turned *Monaco* to starboard, red-to-red: she would pass quite close. Close enough for everyone to see. The ferry was packed with islanders heading off for Christmas who gazed down in curiosity at *Monaco*'s deck. The divers had dressed for the occasion. Frilly knickers, lacy black bras, suspender belts and hairy legs in fishnet stockings were Christmas attire for the men of *Monaco*'s decks.

Carefully watching the still waters of the Sound, I stood by the gunwale under the wheelhouse window. Six fluorescent orange surface marker buoys bobbed about like little hats; each floated above a couple of divers showing us exactly where they were and where not to go. It was mild and sunny on the first morning's dive, calm and still, and above the steady throb of *Monaco*'s engine I could hear a waterfall and the liquid bubbling notes of a curlew. Suddenly I realised I felt almost happy. Connor liked *Monaco*. He appreciated her sophisticated manoeuvrability and was most definitely in charge; everyone knew he was the boss; he simply had an air of authority. I had been right. The divers, well trained by the RAF, were disciplined, good natured and experienced. I wondered about Hugo and what John would be up to, but it felt like years since the responsibilities had been shared, years since I had been able to take the competence and cheerfulness of *Monaco*'s skipper for granted.

Something hit the top of my head. Ouch! Connor hung out of the window directly above, coffee mug in hand. 'I suppose further comment's unnecessary?' enquired the soft Irish voice with a twinkle. More coffee was needed.

He quickly became at home on board. His entertaining Irish wit, ready grin and relaxed approach had spread an air of confidence. We even managed to get out of the sound, round near Staffa on the exposed west side of Mull, where the lads had been able to dive the *Aurania*: a Cunard liner launched in 1916.

She'd been torpedoed by a submarine and was tucked close into the shore. The wreck was tidal and the site exposed at any time of year: in December it was a coup to reach and to dive. It was also a place I loved. I loved the loneliness, the brooding black basalt cliffs looming high above, whose columns seemed to grow out of the smooth sheep-grazed grassy slopes that swept up from the rocky shore. There was no path or track round here and it was a truly isolated and lonely spot. Black chuffs with their red beaks floated above the cliffs, their harsh croaks just audible whilst the sea surged and broke with the swell.

Connor, competent and correct under his casual air, completed the *Monaco*'s log each evening with the statistics for the day: where *Monaco* had been, which dives had been done and in what conditions. He had also added a new a section to the log entitled 'Thought for the Day'. On New Year's Day the entry had read, 'Today I have no thoughts.'

His final entry was, 'And on the Sixth Day God made Woman, and neither he nor Man have had a day's rest since.'

Nineteen

John and I had each handled Digby's death in our own way, and dealing with our own unhappinesses had created a gulf between us. Whatever the divide, whatever the future might be for us, I knew the *Monaco* and Kate and Cubby had saved my sanity. It was over a year since John and the other directors had agreed that *Monaco* and the whole business should be sold. I had bookings and deposits for charters more than eighteen months ahead and of course *Monaco* still had the coveted St Kilda contract, so John felt it made a saleable package. He had found an agent with fancy offices in a smart marina called Ocean Village on the south coast at Southampton where *Monaco* was to be berthed as a convenient viewing place for potential purchasers.

In late July we were ready to wave goodbye to Oban. I was surprised by how many people came to say goodbye and wish me well. Kate was happy. She had an interview coming up with CalMac as she'd applied to be pier master. I knew she'd get the job. Whether it was one of Oban's diminishing fishing fleet or an immaculate mahogany yacht which had just sailed in, she knew how to handle them all and would revel in telling them where to tie up and what dues they had to pay. She'd do it well.

No sign of Cubby. I had wondered if he had heard it was all coming to an end. The note had been tucked into my pocket for days but I'd lacked the courage to find out where he was.

Now we were going and just a spring held *Monaco* on to the North Pier; the engine throbbed purposefully.

'Just a moment,' I shouted up to the open wheel-house window. 'I've got to drop something off before we go.' Jumping up onto the gunwale, I scrambled up the ladder and dashed across the car park into the Oban Inn.

'Could you please pop this behind the bar and give it to Cubby next time he's in,' I said breathlessly to the barman, pushing the crumpled envelope across the bar.

'There'll be no need for that. You can give it to him yourself, he's just over there by the window.' With the light behind him, I'd not noticed him. Turning, I looked across the flagged floor: the light silhouetted his tousled curls. I couldn't find a word.

'Hello there.' His liquid west coast voice flowed through the bar. 'Are you off just now or have you time for a coffee?'

They were all waiting on board, everything was ready, there was only one rope left to cast off and we needed to make use of the tide — but I didn't hesitate a second. 'Of course I'd love a coffee.' And I tucked myself in beside him on the little window seat.

We'd never seen each other or spoken since the day

of the Americans' charter, since John had taken him down to his mother's. I'd always thought he knew, in spite of the Tribunal, in spite of all of our squabbles, I wanted him back. I wanted the original Cubby, the one I had first admired. I had hoped and hoped he would come sauntering along the quay one day to jump lightly on board. My careful enquiries had led me nowhere: no one knew where he was or what he was up to. None of that mattered now. I wanted him to know I understood. I wanted him to know about the reliable, trustworthy *Monaco*, the *Monaco* with no faltering engine, and I wanted him to know about my 'ticket'. Cosily squeezed together on the window seat we chatted happily and easily. But I really did have to go.

'Cubby, it's really so very good to see you. What are you up to? What are your plans?'

I wasn't too sure I really wanted to know, but I couldn't help myself from asking. Typically, he stretched across the table, reaching for the Rizla tin and from amongst the tobacco shreds pulled out an already-rolled thin little cigarette. I grinned; he always knew how to get the most from a moment.

I stood up, pressing on. 'I'm not sure if I'll be back but good luck with whatever you're up to and thank you for all you've taught me.' I bent and kissed him, on his little moustache just beside his lips.

'Aye, well.' He paused, the soft brown eyes looking up at me. 'I'll tell you one thing—' I held my breath. 'You don't bear a grudge!'

Thoughtfully I walked along the quay, making my way

back to *Monaco*. I had never wanted to be the skipper. All I had wanted was to help Kate and Cubby, plan the cruises, and introduce people to the glories of the west coast. I loved telling them about the islands, the history, seabirds and flowers. But somehow it had all gone wrong. Digby's death, Cubby leaving and John's unexpected inheritance had changed everything. And yet it had been a success: people had loved their time on board. They had revelled in the remote islands and lochs, walked on beaches, seen birds and whales they'd never even known existed. No one had lost any money. I had made it work.

But what of my 'ticket'? A Class V with Command Endorsement, what good would that do me? Even now I didn't want to take on the challenges of the Irish Sea, rounding Land's End, or have to deal with the busy shipping lanes of the Channel.

In charge in the wheelhouse was a tobacco-chewing Dane; he'd worked for me before and was an excellent skipper. He got on with the job, had plenty of experience further afield than simply the west coast and was safe. He didn't speak much and usually it was in Danish, unless using the VHF. Hugo had christened him 'Talknot'.

In addition to Hugo and me, on board were Steve and Bob. Over the years both had regularly brought winter dive groups and this voyage right down the west side of England offered an opportunity to thank them. There'd be no atmosphere or wistful ending with these two.

Monaco cruised smoothly south out of Oban bay. Passing the Garvellachs, so romantically named 'the isles of the sea', she swept across the entrance to the Corryvreckan. All was sunny and peaceful, and there were little more than swirling eddies between Scarba and Jura. Oban and all the years there slipped away astern and the island chains stretched into the mist ahead, pretty, gentle and inviting. I could just make out the white block of the hotel at Crinan like a doll's house off to port. I pushed back the memories of that fishy phone box by the pub where I had paused to ring John so many years ago. It had been good to see Cubby again; I hadn't realised how much I had missed his reassuring experience. What would he do now, I wondered.

Early next morning we nudged into the bustling little port of Howth. Unlike Scotland where her green hull was deemed curious, here in Ireland there were lots of green fishing boats, so she simply fitted in. As instructed by the harbour master, we tied up in deep water just inside the entrance and the lads were quickly ashore to check out the Guinness. Talknot stayed on board happily chewing a wad of tobacco as he waited for the fuel tanker, while Hugo and I made a dash for Dublin. I'd promised him a look at the Book of Kells. After all, it had come from Scotland and he had been to Iona and knew all about the exquisite lettering: it appealed to his sense of draughtsmanship. To me it seemed a warm link with Scotland.

In the soft evening light *Monaco* slipped out of Howth again heading south further and further away from her home waters. And yet once she had fished in the Arctic. Enough of this sentimental nonsense! Our next destination would be the Scilly Isles. When *Monaco* had been little more than an idea, John and I had gone through the proposed deck plans and diagrams with our sailing friends in Cornwall, asking their views and advice. Now, I wanted a final bit of fun, to show her off – the finished, working article. I knew they thought she didn't exist, was just a whim, a fantasy. Maybe someone there might like her enough to buy her.

The deck was smooth, the scrubbed planking a bleached silvery white as I wandered towards her stem, past the shiny white Viking life rafts one on each shoulder, past the neatly coiled orange plaited ropes Cubby had found washed up on the west side of Skye. The hatch with its brass portholes letting light and air into accommodation was propped open: no vile stench came wafting out, the picture was still clear in my mind of Cubby breaking the planking with the fire axe so long ago in Troon.

I ducked into the engine room for a reassuring check. Here was my friendly red dragon steadily chugging away; I adjusted the lever to keep the dragon at the right temperature and casually glanced across the top of the engine as I climbed back up the ladder. It was just habit now to check the nearest sight glass.

Clear!

CLEAR!

How could it be clear? The other three were clear too. Not a hint of pinkness. No diesel.

In a moment, the engine would stop.

I ran headlong through the crew mess into the wheelhouse shouting, 'Watch out! The engine's going to stop! There's no fuel!'

The phlegmatic Dane, turned, looking at me he carried on chewing. Trying to impress the urgency on him, I continued more quietly, 'There's no fuel. Nothing showing in the sight glasses. They're all clear, nothing. Not a hint of fuel. I don't understand it as there's never been the slightest falter or problem since Colin altered the pipework,' I finished desperately.

Monaco swept on at a steady ten knots, she creamed through the slight swell without a murmur. To port, quite close, was a small rocky island. Didn't he understand there was no FUEL? He pushed the wodge of tobacco into the corner of his cheek.

'*Må ikke ballade, det er* OK.' What was he on about? He knew I didn't speak Danish!

'Don't worry,' came the heavily accented English, 'it's OK. In Ireland there's no such thing as pink diesel, it's all clear!'

Yet one more fright. Another link in the chain of my steadily growing conviction. If my life had to change, if John and I really had come to an end, I would not spend the rest of my life struggling with huge machinery, stinking diesel and wayward skippers, with gales and cold winter weather exacerbated by dicey finances. However, I would need a job. I knew I would have to make my own way in the world and I would need income.

More than that, I needed to be someone, not just a has-been in a pretty cottage propping up hollyhocks. But I knew *Monaco* was not the answer. Like seaweed swirling round a buoy, a new thought floated around in my mind. I knew the west coast's islands, the beaches and cliff paths from Barra Head to the Butt of Lewis. From the twists of West Loch Tarbert cutting through Jura to the stacs of St Kilda, I knew them all. I knew the orchids and puffin colonies, I knew who lived in that tiny white croft, where they set their creels, what their dog was called and where they went to gather the best tatties and sneak a salmon. I determined to make something out of it all. My 'ticket', knowledge of the sea and struggles had been too hard fought to be wasted; they must be worth something.

First the whole business and *Monaco* had to be sold. Did the agent in Southampton have any idea what he was getting? Ocean Village was populated by glossy fiberglass yachts which rarely moved, providing their Ralph Lauren-clad owners with an immaculate posing platform where *Yachting Monthly* could lounge nonchalantly amongst the morning croissants. An eighty-five-foot solid-oak trawler with a thumping two-stroke diesel engine coming nosing through the pontoons would cause a stir. We'd better make sure it was a Saturday morning for maximum effect. But first the Scillies; I wanted to slip into the anchorage between Tresco and Bryher very quietly in the dark. I wanted my friends to wake up to find *Monaco* amongst the French yachts.

The dragon purred on.

www.sandstonepress.com

 facebook.com/SandstonePress/

@SandstonePress